W9-BEM-893

THE STORY BEHIND THE STRIPE

THE
STORY
BEHIND THE
Stripe

A 100-Year History of d'Arenberg

FAY WOODHOUSE

WITH ROWEN OSBORN

INCLUDING 'NOTES FROM THE WINEMAKER' BY CHESTER OSBORN

WILEY

John Wiley & Sons Australia, Ltd

First published in 2012 by John Wiley & Sons Australia, Ltd
42 McDougall St, Milton Qld 4064
Office also in Melbourne

Typeset in Adobe Caslon 10/16pt

© d'Arenberg Pty Ltd and Fay Woodhouse 2012

The moral rights of the authors have been asserted.

National Library of Australia Cataloguing-in-Publication data

Author:	Woodhouse, Fay.
Title:	The Story Behind the Stripe: A 100-Year History of d'Arenberg/ Fay Woodhouse, Chester Osborn and Rowen Osborn.
ISBN:	9781118231630 (hbk.)
Notes:	Includes bibliographical references and index.
Subjects:	Osborn family
	d'Arenberg Vineyard and Winery—History.
	Vineyards—South Australia—McLaren Vale—History.
	Wine and wine making—South Australia—McLaren Vale—History.
	McLaren Vale Region (S. Aust.)—History.
	South Australia—Genealogy.
Other Authors/Contributors:	Osborn, Chester.
	Osborn, Rowen.
Dewey Number:	663.20099423

Cover and internal design by saso content & design pty limited

Photo credits:
Section 1: p. 1 (top left): courtesy Norwood Football Club; p. 1 (top right and bottom): courtesy Barr Smith Special Collection, Adelaide University.
Section 2: p. 4 (top) and p. 7 (top): photographs by John Kruger.
All other photographs: d'Arenberg records and archives.

Printed in Singapore by
Markono Print Media Pte Ltd

10 9 8 7 6 5 4 3 2 1

Disclaimer
The material in this publication is of the nature of general comment only, and does not represent professional advice. It is not intended to provide specific guidance for particular circumstances and it should not be relied on as the basis for any decision to take action or not take action on any matter which it covers. Readers should obtain professional advice where appropriate, before making any such decision. To the maximum extent permitted by law, the authors and publisher disclaim all responsibility and liability to any person, arising directly or indirectly from any person taking or not taking action based on the information in this publication.

Foreword

THROUGHOUT THE WORLD OF WINE THERE ARE WINERIES THAT EVOLVE to embody the very essence of their place. These wineries not only make exemplary wines that often set the agenda for their entire region, but they are an inseparable and important part of the spirit of that place, a spirit that has inevitably taken shape over multiple generations.

d'Arenberg is one of these.

Australia is still a relatively young and developing nation when it comes to many things, not least of all wine. Scattered across the country, mostly young vines grow in ancient soils and most winemakers are eking out their first and second vinous incarnations.

But d'Arenberg is one winery with roots that run deeper into time and into the development of McLaren Vale the place, one of only a handful of wine regions with a real sense of history in Australia. Here, among an outcrop of ancient vines, framed by rolling hills and spectacular coastline, is the playground of the Osborn family.

The Osborns' deep understanding of where they live, grow grapes and make wine and how they came to be doing what they do so well is something they carry effortlessly with them.

And today's wine-adoring world is full of people who have either visited this iconic McLaren Vale winery or have been visited by the winery in their part of the world. An encounter with d'Arenberg, whether on their soil or yours, leaves you with a lasting impression of a winery and a family that have created something both unique and engaging.

And where great wineries exist, those that are the flag bearers for their entire region, you'll inevitably find strong personalities and memorable characters driving them along.

For it is one thing to make great wine that taps deep into *terroir*, culture and carefully nurtured tradition, but to then bring it to life in far-flung places as convincingly as on home soil requires both gifted storytelling skills and relentless hard work.

Both d'Arry and Chester Osborn have established themselves as widely respected, indeed famous winemakers in their respective generations, but they are both also great storytellers and this talent cannot be overestimated. It has grown to become an integral part of the d'Arenberg spirit and, now famously, each bottle bears its own colourful tale.

The blood of the Australian larrikin runs thick in the Osborns, with irrepressible charm and a constant eye for enjoyment. Things are serious in the vineyard and winery and ribald around open bottles.

They are an astute international winemaking success story, canny business people and they have one eye keenly trained on the future, the other diligently focused on what has gone before.

The balance between tradition and innovation is one of the hardest things to get right in today's wine business and yet here is a family and winery with an innate feel for this.

On the one hand, there is a constant and intensive search for inspiration that really knows no bounds, looking to other cultures and continents.

Then there is the dutiful service to home turf, assessing what is available, knowing where each kaleidoscopic fragment best fits and what must be done to improve things.

With their established and revered tradition comes a custodial responsibility — one of the greatest challenges in today's wine business.

But for d'Arenberg this ability to take care of what's come before is written into their DNA. They have effortless charm, an eye for making an honest glass of wine, a feel for how things local sit in the international context and an unquenchable curiosity for making an important contribution.

It is rare, anywhere in the world, to find a winery like d'Arenberg that combines value, variety and consistency with such conviction. Over successive generations of continuous hard work they have earned the right to represent their region's beauty, uniqueness and innate sense for laid-back enjoyment.

They have shaped McLaren Vale and the place is better for it, as are all of us who count ourselves as lovers of great Australian wine. We are lucky to count d'Arenberg among our own.

NICK STOCK

William Osborn (1826–1907) married Elizabeth Rowe (1828–1907)
All Saints' Church, Lambeth, London, 21 July 1851

Joseph Rowe
(31 January 1852–25 May 1921)
m. Mary Jane Turnbull Stewart
(11 September 1862–17 March 1957)

William Francis
(16 September 1853–29 April 1936)

Mary Jane
(25 September 1858–30 October 1860)

Mary Elizabeth
(21 April 1884–1970)
m. James Marshall, 1909 (d. 1946)

Edward
(1885–1888)

Francis Ernest (Frank)
(15 April 1888–3 August 1957)
m. Helena d'Arenberg, 1920 (d. 1926)

Edith Florence
(21 February 1891–7 September 1981)
m. 1. Theo Felstead, 1914 (d. 1918)
m. 2. Samuel Elderton Tolley, 1920 (d. 1966)

Jane Antoinette (Toni)
b. 9 September 1921
m. Patrick William Bourne, 1958 (d. 1995)

Rowen Frederick
b. 10 November 1924
m. Beverley Jean Gemmell, 1956

Francis d'Arenberg (d'Arry)
b. 27 December 1926
m. Pauline Preston, 1958 (d. 2002)

Christopher Francis
b. 1 June 1958

Timothy Andrew
b. 5 September 1960

Elizabeth Jane
b. 9 October 1967
m. Antony Ross Allen, 2001

Jacqueline Helena
b. 22 July 1959

Chester d'Arenberg
b. 1 July 1962
m. Bernadette Wieland, 1996

b. John Osborn Allan, 2003
b. Nicolas Osborn Allan, 2006

Alicia, b. 12 September 1996
Ruby, b. 20 October 1999
Mia, b. 22 April 2003

Contents

About the authors

Fay Woodhouse

Dr Fay Woodhouse is a historian, researcher and biographer. She has a strong background in Australian and Victorian history. Her latest books include *Leslie Latham: A Biography* (2011), *Vintage Stories: A 150 Year History of Tahbilk* (2010), *Altona Yacht Club: A History of Community Sailing* (2010), *Working for Welfare: A History of the Australian Institute of Welfare and Community Workers* (2010) and *Still Learning: A 50 Year History of Monash University Peninsula Campus* (2008). With historian Peter Yule, she is currently writing the 50-year history of the Faculty of Law, Monash University. Fay is the Victorian Researcher for *The Australian Dictionary of Biography* and is an Honorary Research Fellow in the School of Historical and Philosophical Studies, University of Melbourne.

Rowen Osborn

Rowen Frederick Osborn (born 1924) is the oldest son of Frank and Helen Osborn. He spent his entire career as an Australian diplomat. Educated at Prince Alfred College and the University of Adelaide, as an External Affairs cadet Rowen was appointed Third Secretary to the Australian High Commission, Karachi, Pakistan. He later served as External Affairs Officer and Second Secretary, Australian Embassy, The Hague; Second Secretary and later Secretary, Australian Embassy, Tokyo; Counsellor, Australian High Commission, London; Head, Office of Current Intelligence, Joint Intelligence Organisation; First Assistant Secretary, Minister, Australian Embassy, Tokyo; and Australian High Commissioner, Ottawa, Canada. He was a Member of the Australian Delegations to the United Nations XI General Assembly, New York 1956–57. Since retiring from the Commonwealth Public Service in 1985, Rowen has indulged his interest in his own family's history. He published *J R Osborn and his Racehorses* in 2001.

Acknowledgements

THE IMPETUS FOR THE PUBLICATION OF THIS HISTORY OF d'ARENBERG WINES was the desire to celebrate and acknowledge one hundred years of winemaking by the Osborn family in McLaren Vale. This book has been a collaborative work. The intricate early family history could not have been assembled without the expert, time-consuming and enthusiastic research undertaken over decades by Rowen Osborn. As an Australian diplomat for more than 40 years, his postings in Europe and around the world allowed him to visit many archives and libraries to discover what he could about the Australian d'Arenberg family and their European connections. I take this opportunity to pay tribute to Rowen's superb work and thank him for it, and to acknowledge his assistance to me in editing and reworking his drafted family history.

I would also like to express my sincere thanks to the wonderful archivists and historians whose efforts in uncovering information have added to the depth of this history. I thank Andrew Cook, Archives Officer at the University of Adelaide, for photographs of Frank Osborn; Katie Wood, Coordinator, Archives Reference, University of Melbourne Archives, for locating Frank's student record; Tony Aldous, School Archivist, Prince Alfred College, for his enthusiastic response to my queries as well as photographs and relevant copies of the *Chronicle*; Emma Greenwood, Librarian, Trinity Laban Conservatoire of Music and Dance,

Acknowledgements

London, for her search for records of Helena d'Arenberg; historian Michael Coligan, and Richmond Football Club historian and MCC Assistant Librarian Trevor Ruddell, for information regarding Joe Osborn's football career in Victoria; Faye Lush, Librarian, Willunga National Trust, for local photographs; and Helen Bruce, Reference Archivist, the University of Adelaide, for her research into Helena d'Arenberg's enrolment at the Adelaide Conservatorium. I would especially like to thank my colleague Dr David Dunstan, of Monash University and *The Australian Dictionary of Biography*, for his valuable assistance and advice, and encouragement in telling the d'Arenberg story.

To the publishing team at John Wiley & Sons, I extend my thanks to Lucy Raymond, Clare Weber, Dani Karvess and Elizabeth Whiley. Special thanks go to Wiley's editor, Jem Bates.

And without the support of the Osborn family and the wonderful staff at d'Arenberg my work would have been very difficult indeed. To d'Arry and Chester Osborn, Luke Tyler, Philip Jeffries, Phoebe LeMessurier, Lincoln Ridley and Zoe Ottaway, many thanks.

FAY WOODHOUSE

Introduction

S EEDS OF THE 'CLARET' GRAPE, SO WE ARE TOLD, AND SEVERAL ROOTED VINES were among the many shrubs and plants carried to New South Wales by the 11 ships of the First Fleet; they were planted in Sydney Cove by Captain Arthur Phillip within a few days of arrival. The climate and location meant the vines did not prosper. More vines were sent for and planted at Rose Hill, now Parramatta, where they did thrive. Lieutenant John Macarthur was among those who perceived that wine growing could 'civilise' the New South Wales penal colony. A vineyard was planted around 1820 at Camden Park by Macarthur and his sons, James and William. This became the first commercial vineyard in New South Wales when William produced 250 gallons of wine from one acre in 1830; the wine later brought overseas acclaim. James Busby, however, must be acknowledged as the founder of the Australian wine industry as we know it today. His contribution to our knowledge and understanding of wine was vast. Busby's *Treatise on the Culture of the Vine*, published in 1825, and his second book, *A Manual of Plain Directions for Planting and Cultivating Vineyards and for Making Wine*, provided prospective colonial winemakers with exacting instructions and the benefit of his experience.

While winemaking began in New South Wales, the race for British sovereignty over the southern 'wastelands' of Australia created an urgency to settle the land beyond. South Australia was proclaimed a province by Governor Captain John Hindmarsh on 28 December 1836. Six months earlier, eight ships had arrived in South Australia carrying officials and settlers accompanied by livestock, goods and chattels. Edward Gibbon Wakefield had originally published a pamphlet proposing a system of settlement by which land would be sold to men of capital. His idea was that the proceeds from these initial sales should go towards funding the passage of free selected emigrants, the young and healthy who would provide a pool of labour and have an incentive to buy land of their own. The Industrial Revolution had generated widespread poverty, unemployment and social unrest, and Wakefield's idea appealed to a group of influential individuals who considered it a viable solution to England's growing problems. The South Australian Association was formed in London in 1833; the South Australian Colonization Bill was introduced into the House of Lords and on 15 August 1834 it received the King's assent.[1] Two other striking aspects of Wakefield's ideas were that no convicts should be transported to South Australia, and that land should be sold at prices of at least 12 shillings per acre (although in practice the price was later lowered). The South Australian Company was formed and completely dominated settlement of the province. South Australia came into being as the 'largest and most ambitious exercise in private enterprise the world had seen'.[2] This antipodean utopia was initially populated by small-time capitalists, sons of the landed gentry, industrious adventurers and large numbers of willing emigrants — 7000 in all had arrived by the end of 1836. When we trace the origins of the earliest owners of what is now d'Arenberg vineyards and winery, a snapshot of these early emigrants is revealed.

Early South Australian winemakers

In the first 10 years of settlement many of the districts within a 60-mile radius of Adelaide were opened up. The land was cleared and the Aboriginal tribes were dispossessed. Although England was not a wine-producing country, the determination of the ruling few to ensure a supply of wine from antipodean vineyards proved to be an incentive to establish an Australian wine industry.

The first South Australian vineyards were planted in 1837 by John Barton Hack, who propagated cuttings he had obtained in Launceston. But it was the winemakers John Reynell, Alexander Kelly and Thomas Hardy who were crucial to the establishment of the South Australian wine industry. John Reynell, who arrived in South Australia in 1838, planted vines he had brought from the Cape of Good Hope. By 1839 there were 60 varieties of grapes in the colony including Riesling, Cabernet, Shiraz, Tokay, Verdelho, Malbec, Grenache, Carignane and Mataro. At a public meeting in 1840 it was resolved to import 500 000 vines from the Cape of Good Hope. In 1845 Reynell obtained vine cuttings from John Macarthur in Camden, New South Wales, and established the first commercial vineyard in South Australia. In 1876 Reynell died at the age of 67; his sons and their children built one of the first intergenerational wine families in Australia.

Dr Alexander Kelly, a physician and great advocate of wine, was quick to see the colony's potential for wine production; he planted the 'Trinity' vineyard in about 1842 and the 'Tintara' vineyard in 1863.[3] Kelly wrote two seminal books on wine, *The Vine in Australia* (1861) and *Wine Growing in Australia* (1867). Among other growing techniques, he introduced the use of contour planting to

prevent soil erosion. While he exhibited great foresight in the development of an Australian industry, he was not an astute businessman. 'Tintara' was hit by the 1860 Depression and declared bankrupt by 1873, despite its full cellars. The company was purchased by winemaker Thomas Hardy, the only bidder. Thomas, with his three sons, James, Thomas and Nathaniel, established a successful business and formed a partnership in 1887, Thomas Hardy & Sons Limited. They soon became the largest exporter of wine to the United Kingdom. When Thomas Hardy junior died in 1912, Joseph Osborn was company secretary and a director of Thomas Hardy & Sons.

Terroir

What Reynell, Kelly and Hardy all had in common was their belief that the characteristics required for successful grape growing and wine production were present in the McLaren Vale landscape they were drawn to. Max Lake discusses the importance of *terroir* (although he does not use this term) in his 1966 volume, *Classic Wines of Australia*, in which he admires the 'knowledge and skill of the men who chose these lands a century or more ago, when the virgin country comprised stands of timber and grassland'. The pioneer winemakers of the district chose the McLaren Vale for its suitable soils and climate. The best Australian growths, according to Lake, come from vines that receive the most morning sun. The best reds are grown mainly on the hills and slopes with clay subsoil and plenty of calcareous matter, the whites principally on either flats or lighter soil hills and slopes.[4] The

French refer to the distinct blend of soil and climate in winemaking districts as *terroir*, a word for which no precise English translation exists. *Terroir* has a number of components including the composition of the surface soil and subsoil, the soil structure, and the local topography (altitude, slope and aspect). It also includes climate as measured by temperature and rainfall. As Jancis Robinson notes, the main emphasis in nearly all French wine writing is on the soil, and especially its role and interactions with other elements of the environment in governing water supply to the vine.[5] Max Lake emphasises the differences in *terroir* among the many distinct wine-producing districts of Australia. He contrasts regional characteristics and soil variation, citing examples as diverse as the rich red soils of Coonawarra, the impact of volcanic activity on Hunter region vineyards, the rich, silty alluvial deposits of Langhorne Creek, and the gravel knob and mixture of ironstone with medium loam topsoil in parts of McLaren Vale. Today individual vineyards within wine regions may be distinguished by their own distinct *terroir*.

In recognition of the wide range of Australian wine regions, the industry has now formally defined and described its viticultural landscapes. In the Australian Geographical Indications (GI) contained in the Register of Protected Names, the GI of McLaren Vale is categorised under the Fleurieu Peninsula GI.

Understanding McLaren Vale's diverse *terroir* has been a multi-generational mission for the Osborn family. The original property alone ranges from red earth clay on limestone to sand on marly limestone to grey loam on clay. The changing soil type and quality of soil along with the influence of aspect and altitude were some of the first lessons passed between father and son. The diversity of *terroir* within the d'Arenberg vineyards is currently managed and nurtured lovingly by

fourth-generation winemaker and viticulturalist Chester Osborn. With vineyards now grown and contracted outside the estate and stretching to all corners of the region, this understanding of the land has taken on new meaning. Soil samples and recent geological exploration help fill the gaps, but nothing can replace experience and trial and error. It's a lifelong pursuit as each vintage throws up new challenges and more information, and the process starts again with each variety introduced. Over the past 25 years Chester has slowly incorporated old-world, labour-intensive techniques into his winemaking practice. d'Arenberg's use of open fermentation, foot treading and basket pressing helps preserve the primary fruit characters to create structured wines that age well. Concerned not only for the sustainability of the land but also for the sustainability of the vines, Chester ceased fertilising the vineyards more than a decade ago.

As a winemaking region, McLaren Vale has long been a powerhouse of Australian wine exports, and today the Osborns are among the best-known and most established growers and exporters of wine from this celebrated wine region. McLaren Vale, with a winemaking history dating back 150 years, has as much integrity and history as the other great winemaking regions of the world.

Family tradition

When Frank Osborn began Bundarra Vineyards he grew grapes for sale to the large McLaren Vale producers, but he soon decided to enter the winemaking business himself. Guided by his brother-in-law and mentor, Sam Tolley (of Tolley,

Scott & Tolley, wine and brandy makers), benefiting from hands-on winemaking experience with the Wilkinsons of Ryecroft, and encouraged by his friends and neighbours, Frank began to produce bulk wine in 1928 specifically for the export market. It was the right move at a pivotal time in Australian winemaking history.

Born into a fledgling winemaking family, Frank's second son d'Arry knew from an early age that he too wanted to become a winemaker. In the early 1940s, when d'Arry left school early to help his father in the vineyard, he was helped and encouraged by Cud Kay of Kay Brothers among others. When d'Arry decided to bottle and produce his own label, he was supported by friends and neighbours in the new venture. d'Arry had already established lasting friendships with many of the winemakers of the day, including locals Geoff Merrill, James Ingoldby, Ben Chaffey and, in Victoria, Eric Purbrick. He continued the winemaking tradition begun by his father, first making burgundies in the way his father had, then adding Cabernet Sauvignons to his portfolio, which soon began winning awards at wine shows, including the 1969 Jimmy Watson Award for the best one-year-old red.

d'Arry's son Chester knew at seven years old that he, in turn, would become a winemaker. Over the past 30 years father and son have taken the d'Arenberg name to exalted heights in the wine world. Today Chester is one of the country's most innovative and celebrated winemakers, a talented viticulturalist who consistently pushes the boundaries.

Intergenerational winemaking families populate the Australian wine landscape. The Osborns are one of the dozen families who, in 2006, formed a collective known as the Australia's First Families of Wine (AFFW) to showcase the generations of expertise the Australian wine industry has to offer and can be proud of. This collective has been highly successful in marketing and distributing their wine around the world. That the Osborn family should play a key role in this group is part of the story of the d'Arenberg stripe.

Writing a family history and a business history

Writing the history of a family requires a biographer to employ distinct skills and sensitivities. Writing the history of a business enterprise may take the historian into numerous interrelated research areas, where it is easy to become diverted. This centennial history of d'Arenberg Wines introduces five generations of two families over 100 years, a substantial time span. In attempting to create an authentic portrait of the family against the backdrop of the growing family business and the evolving Australian wine industry, I have tried to draw together the various strands of the story into an engaging and integrated whole.

When Rowen Osborn began researching the little-known history of his Osborn and d'Arenberg forebears decades ago, he had no access to the tools that allow today's researcher to retrieve birth, death and marriage certificates, for instance, almost instantly. Until relatively recently back issues of *The Times* newspaper had to be found and consulted; letters had to be sent to Australia House in London, and to university and other archives; and any, much-anticipated answers might be received months later. Today this work can be completed much more simply. Yet despite all the groundwork laid by Rowen, and my own further extensive research, a few missing pieces remain. Consulting various school, university and

newspaper archives revealed answers to many of the questions I had accumulated as I progressed in this project. Sadly, answers to some of the deeper historical mysteries, especially relating to the fascinating origins of the d'Arenberg family, remain elusive.

The history of the Osborn family and the story of F E Osborn & Sons and d'Arenberg Wines are inextricably linked to the development of the wine industry in Australia. Today the Osborns are one of Australia's leading family-owned wine businesses and their wines are sought after by connoisseurs and interested amateurs all over the world. Chester Osborn is truly one of Australia's masters of the winemaker's art. This family business has been synonymous with Australians themselves becoming wine drinkers, something that only happened after the Second World War.

As it celebrates its 100-year history, d'Arenberg operates as a medium-sized business while retaining its distinct feeling of being a family-owned wine company. The story of d'Arenberg, the creation of the d'Arenberg stripe, the label and the wines with their quirky names, is a story well worth telling.

CHAPTER 1

The Osborns of McLaren Vale

So enthusiastic was he about his future prospects that, before his arrival in McLaren Vale in April 1912, Frank Osborn already described himself as a 'vigneron'. This was something of a pre-emptive strike for the 24 year old. The occupation was chosen because Frank and his father, Joseph, had purchased a vineyard from the Milton family in December 1911. Acquiring this property was the beginning of a new life and career for Frank who, after failing medicine at both Adelaide University and the University of Melbourne, had no real qualifications and no obvious career prospects. Perhaps the most striking characteristic of the would-be vigneron was that he was a keen sportsman; he especially prided himself as a cricketer. He eventually proved to be a real sport in the wine industry too. After Frank's spectacular failure as a medico, however, his father knew that he needed a different form of employment. So Joseph, who had worked in the wine industry for Thomas Hardy & Sons for 30 years, decided Frank should make a go of grape growing. The Milton property had been producing grapes since 1891 and selling them for the overseas market. Thomas Hardy had established his own business in McLaren Vale in 1853, but it was not until 1878 that he encouraged farmers in the region to turn to grape growing and the fledgling industry took off. Between 1880 and 1890 more than 300 000 vines were planted in McLaren Vale. The area was well suited to vines because of the climate, rainfall and the abundance of suitable soils. William Milton grew grapes successfully for 20 years, selling them to Thomas Hardy and Tatachilla. After he died in 1905 his children continued winemaking but they decided to sell the property in 1911. It was a perfect opportunity for Frank to prove himself to his father, whose own career had been varied, to say the least.

Who were the Osborns? — a little family history

But, to understand how Joseph and Frank Osborn arrived at that critical moment in 1912, we need to take a brief detour into Osborn family history. Purchasing the Milton property was a step into the unknown for the Osborns, but when we look at the history of Joseph's own parents, perhaps it is unsurprising that the Australian family were prepared to take risks. As we shall see, although Joseph worked in the wine industry, he had no practical experience of grape growing. And he was a teetotaller. His son, Frank, although enthusiastic, came to the venture without any applicable experience, simply harbouring a desire to go onto the land. Perhaps his forebears' humble origins in Cornwall had some bearing on the matter. Their stories illustrate a desire for a better life and a preparedness to travel from one side of the world to the other to find it.

William Osborn senior (c. 1826–1882)

William Osborn was the first of the Osborn family to arrive in Australia. Born in Cornwall in about 1826, he became a cordwainer, or shoemaker, and this was how he supported himself in Victoria. William was the son of a carpet-weaver, also William, and Elizabeth Rowe, who had married at All Saints' Church, Lambeth, on 21 July 1851. Their sons were born in Truro, Cornwall—Joseph Rowe Osborn at Boscawer Bridge on 31 January 1852, William Francis Osborn on St Austell Street on 16 September 1853. News of gold discoveries in New South Wales and Victoria in 1851 was the catalyst for the migration of thousands of Cornish miners and mining hopefuls to travel to the Australian colonies. William Osborn travelled out to Australia as an unassisted passenger (that is, without the aid of a government subsidy) in August 1854 on the *Morning Star* to join his brother-in-law, Cornelius Tippet, who had left England as an assisted passenger just two months earlier on the *Conway* on 29 June 1854. The family suspect that, like many migrants of the day, the men had an understanding with their wives that once they had arrived and settled they would see whether they could make a future for themselves in Melbourne. Perhaps, like thousands of others, William and Cornelius tried their luck in the goldfields and, like so many, they were unsuccessful. Most would-be miners lasted only six weeks on the diggings then gave up. Given their trades, and the great need for labour of every kind in Melbourne, the pair probably returned to the metropolis and found work easily.

William is listed in the *Melbourne & Suburbs Directories* as a boot- and shoemaker in Bridge Road, Richmond, between 1859 and 1866–67, 10 years after his wife,

Elizabeth, arrived. His marriage with Elizabeth was ultimately unsuccessful. He left Melbourne and in 1882 was working as a groom at the Royal Victorian Hotel at Wangaratta. William Osborn died by drowning in the nearby Ovens River on 20 November 1882. A magistrate's inquiry found there was no evidence as to whether the drowning was accidental or premeditated. A report in the Melbourne press highlighted his early career, confirming that 'he was some years ago in a large way of business in the boot trade in Melbourne'; the suggestion that he once stood as a candidate for the Assembly cannot be corroborated, although as a property owner he was eligible to stand. William died intestate and Letters of Administration were granted to Elizabeth on 3 August 1885.

Elizabeth Osborn (née Rowe) (1828–1907)

Elizabeth Osborn (née Rowe) was born in Tregony, Cornwall, on 25 December 1828 and was baptised in the ancient church of St Cuby in the village. She was the daughter of Frances Rowe, a bricklayer, and his wife, Elizabeth. Her siblings were Lucy (born in 1823), Joseph (1825), Francis (1831), Thomasine (1834) and James (1837). Elizabeth, then aged 29, and her 34-year-old sister, Lucy, together with Elizabeth's children, Joseph (aged 5) and William (4), left Plymouth on the *Medway* as assisted migrants on 16 September 1857 and arrived in Melbourne on 19 December. In the captain's log, Elizabeth is described as housekeeper; her religion and that of the boys Wesleyan. The Assisted Migrant Register noted that she would be joining her husband at Cornwall House, Bridge Road, Richmond, and that both she and Joseph could read and write. Following the family's reunion, Mary Jane Osborn was born on 25 September 1858. The infant died at Richmond on 30 October 1860 and was buried in the Melbourne Cemetery.

Lucy Rowe (1823–1906) married Cornelius Tippet, a wood turner; her occupation is noted in the ship's log as seamstress. In 1859 Lucy is listed in the *Melbourne & Suburbs Directories* in a dressmaking and millinery business with Mrs Clifton at 30 Russell Street, Melbourne; her husband was a general wood turner at 218 Bourke Street East. By 1866 the Tippets were living at 67 Highett Street, Richmond. Cornelius Tippet died on 9 November 1869 at the age of 43; he and Lucy had no children. They appear to have been a very devout couple: the inscription on his gravestone reads 'In sure and certain hope of a glorious resurrection'. Lucy gave Cornelius's Bible, which bears his signature and the date 18 August 1849, to their nephew Joseph Rowe Osborn in 1874. The inscription, 'Presented to J R Osborn by his affectionate Aunt, praying he may make it the guide of his life as did his Dear Uncle C. Tippet', indicates their deep religiosity.[1]

After her husband's death, Lucy Tippet, who lived for the rest of her life in Richmond, turned to a variety of occupations including running a boarding house and once again working as a dressmaker. When she made her will on 28 April 1890, her address was 67 Highett Street.[2] She died on 16 May 1906 at the age of 83 and, as directed by her will, was buried on 19 May in the same grave as her husband. The inscription over her grave, 'A Long Patient Sufferer at Rest', suggests long-term ill health. Lucy appointed her nephew Joseph as her sole executor and trustee. While she was clearly on good terms with her Osborn

nephew, great-nephew and nieces, the nature of Lucy's relationship with her sister Elizabeth and brother-in-law William is less clear. Anecdotal evidence suggests that Elizabeth's relationship with Lucy deteriorated after the death of her husband, Cornelius. In her will, Lucy directed that her executor 'may let my houses to any tenant except his mother'; that is, her sister Elizabeth. This incidentally indicates she had accumulated some wealth during her life in Australia. Although it is evident that Lucy and her sister were not on good terms, the reason for this is unclear. William was known to be living at 67 Highett Street (the same address as his sister-in-law) intermittently before his move to Wangaratta, where he died in 1882. Lucy's estate was to be divided between Joseph's children, Mary, Francis and Edith, when the youngest reached the age of 21 in 1912.

Whatever the relationship between the sisters when they were living, they were united in death: Elizabeth Osborn was buried in the Tippet grave 18 months after her sister. In Elizabeth's case, her inscription reads simply 'Beloved and sadly missed'. When Elizabeth Osborn died on 15 November 1907 'of chronic nephritis', she was living at her son William's home in Richmond. Her death notice in the Melbourne *Age* of 18 November describes her as 'the dearly loved mother of both sons, Joseph Rowe and William Francis', although Joseph and his children seem to have had little contact with her.

The discovery of gold had opened up the colony of Victoria, attracting huge numbers of immigrants from across the world with the hope of a better life. Elizabeth and William Osborn, together with Lucy and Cornelius Tippet, set off into the unknown — took a leap of faith. Their children, William and Joseph, were brought up within the strictures of the Methodist religion, and while of different temperaments, both sons, to varying degrees, fulfilled their personal and professional ambitions.

William Francis Osborn (William Junior) (1853–1936)

Little is known of the early life of William and Elizabeth's younger son, William Francis, except that he married Henrietta Hodder in 1889. She was the daughter of William Charles Hodder and Nancy Hodder (née Paul). Initially a painter in York Street, Emerald Hill (now South Melbourne), Hodder appears to have then relocated to Sloane Street, Stawell, a large gold-mining town in the Wimmera district, 30 miles west of the large regional township of Horsham. This township was also located on the main Melbourne to Adelaide railway line. William Francis Osborn's name appears in the *Melbourne & Suburban Directories* as a draper at Baillie Street, Horsham, from 1888 until 1900. It may be that William met Henrietta in South Melbourne and followed her family to the Wimmera, settling in Horsham where there may have been greater opportunity for employment.

William Osborn junior, it appears, had civic and municipal ambitions. He was a candidate for the Horsham Council in 1889, 1890 and 1891 but was beaten each time. Fortuitously, a resignation following the 1891 elections saw him elected to council that year. He was elected mayor in August 1893 and retired from the council at the expiration of his term two years later. He was a committee member of Horsham Cricket Club in 1886 and club secretary in 1889. He was also on the

committee of the Athletic Club and secretary-treasurer of the Recreation Reserve Committee of Management and secretary of the Horsham Race Club.

William junior's story is sadly incomplete. We do not know what became of him between 1890 and 29 April 1936, when he died at the Bendigo Benevolent Asylum of 'senile decay' at 83 years of age. Although no record has been found of William and Henrietta's divorce (Henrietta lived until 1958), it seems they were at least separated by the time of William's death in 1936. William's and his brother Joseph's lives followed very different paths, as we shall see.

Joseph Rowe Osborn

Born in Truro, Cornwall, in 1852, Joseph Rowe Osborn grew up in Victoria from the age of six. The reunited family settled in Richmond, where Joseph 'acquired a sound education at the Richmond Seminary, under the tutorship of Mr Walker'. On leaving school, he 'entered upon mercantile pursuits', although the nature of these pursuits is unknown.[3]

An enthusiastic patron of the turf

Joseph Osborn loved sport. He was an enthusiastic Australian rules footballer. An article published in the *Freelance and LV Gazette* on 25 May 1901 notes that 'J R Osborn agitated' for the adoption of the 'Victorian' game in the late 1870s.

Joseph played for Richmond from 1871 to 1874 and was club secretary in 1873.[4] After the close of the 1874 football season, at the age of 21, Joseph moved to South Australia, where he captained the Woodville Club, a foundation club of the South Australian Football Association. As a Woodville delegate, Joseph was one of about 80 people who attended an extraordinary meeting at the Prince Alfred Hotel, Adelaide, on 23 April 1877, convened by Bayfield Moulden, with whom Joseph developed a lifelong friendship. The meeting decided to form an association of clubs to be called the South Australian Football Association. A week later delegates considered rules for both the new association and the game. J R Osborn was elected honorary treasurer and also a member of the match committee. Two more weekly meetings were held before a challenge was issued to the Victorian Football Association to play a match in Melbourne. In 1878 Osborn, A J Diamond and H C Burnet founded the Norwood Football Club. Joseph, who retained his connection with the club after his retirement from playing, served as treasurer until 1895.[5]

Joseph was also a very successful racehorse owner, especially in Adelaide and Melbourne. In Sydney between 1895 and 1912 he raced under the name 'J Rowen'. He may have used this name to hide these activities from his mother. Elizabeth Osborn's strong Methodist beliefs probably proscribed indulgence in gambling and drinking, so her son's horse racing activities would have scandalised her. Whatever the explanation, J Rowen's racing colours were 'all canary' and it is said he kept bolts of yellow silk from which jackets and caps were cut for the jockeys. Two racing trophies have survived. The Adelaide Racing Club's Birthday Cup, won by True Scot in 1905, resides proudly at the Osborn house in Canberra.

Another memento, a lady's bracelet engraved 'MEO [Mary Elizabeth Osborn] True Scot 1905' is believed to commemorate True Scot's first win in the Victorian Racing Club's Encourage Handicap for two year olds on 4 November 1905.[6] J Rowen's name appears, with only two exceptions, in the *Australasian Turf Register* from 1895–96 to 1912–13.[7]

On 25 July 1883 Joseph married Mary Jane Turnbull Stewart. Mary, whose family arrived in South Australia from Liverpool, was born in Port Adelaide on 11 September 1862. She was the daughter of a hotelier, Thomas Arthur Stewart. Originally a wheelwright, by 1852 Thomas was the licensee of the Thistle Inn, Port Adelaide. Later he became licensee of the Henley Hotel and then of the Bush Inn, Willunga. Joseph and Mary were married by the Reverend William Fletcher of the Congregational Stow Memorial Church.[8] The newlyweds moved into 'Rochdale' at 39 Rochester Street, Leabrook.

A man of means

In 1908, when Joseph was 56 years old, his biography appeared in the *Cyclopedia of South Australia*. Accompanied by a photograph, it gives a succinct sketch of his life to that date; he either provided the information or wrote it himself. No hint is given as to the nature of his 'mercantile pursuits', how and exactly when he secured an appointment in the Government Audit Office or what he did there. Nevertheless he remained in the Audit Office until 1881, when he joined Thomas Hardy Limited, wine merchants, as company secretary. Three years later, together with Hardy's sons, he became a partner in the firm. He was appointed director when the company was renamed Thomas Hardy and Sons Limited in 1894. In 1908, when the *Cyclopedia* was published, Osborn was secretary and director of the company.[9] His 'very deep interest in the affairs of the district' saw him elected to a seat on the Burnside District Council representing the Burnside ward in 1888, the year his son Frank was born. He was elected chairman of the council in 1892, a position he still held in 1908. Throughout the second part of the biographical article Joseph is referred to as 'Mr Rowen', clearly a reference to his role as racehorse owner. In racing circles it was well known that Joseph Osborn and Mr J Rowen, 'an enthusiastic patron of the turf', were one and the same man.

Joseph Osborn was a teetotaller. As a youth he took the pledge to abstain from alcohol and he did not break this pledge throughout his entire life. The modern reader may find it hard to believe that he remained abstinent, given his credentials as a keen sportsman who was deeply involved in the racing industry, married to the daughter of a hotelier and spent the last 30 years of his working life with Thomas Hardy, wine merchants. Abstinence among those working in the wine industry was not uncommon, however, and teetotallers working in senior positions were highly regarded and greatly trusted by their employers. Rowen, Toni and d'Arry Osborn all confirm that, according to their father, Frank, their grandfather most certainly remained true to his pledge.

Before his marriage, Joseph commissioned the construction of a bluestone house in Rochester Street, Leabrook, now part of the suburb of Burnside, Adelaide. It was a large, stylish, Italianate villa of a type popular and fashionable in the 1880s and an indicator of status and wealth in Adelaide. This was the grand home to which he took his bride and where their children were born. Their eldest child, Mary Elizabeth, was born on 21 April 1884; their second, Edward, was born in 1885 but died on 6 December 1888.[10] Two more children followed: Francis Ernest (Frank) on 15 April 1888 and Edith Florence on 21 February 1891.

The house was built on part of Section 299, Hundred of Adelaide. This was a 134-acre section originally taken up by the South Australian Company in 1838 for £83 15s 0d. Joseph Eldin Moulden (1812–1891) with his sons, Beaumont (1849–1926) and Bayfield Moulden (1854–1933), began the subdivision of Section 299.[11] According to Burnside historian Elizabeth Warburton, 'The Mouldens made almost a hobby out of land development and were concerned in much of the change from rural to suburban living in the eastern suburbs'.[12] The new suburbs were known as Leabrook and Upper Kensington. Most of the blocks were large, with 180-foot frontages and depths of 200 feet or more — the traditional quarter-acre block. Joseph Moulden had practised law in London after completing his articles in the office where Charles Dickens had been an articled clerk. Moulden had a country retreat called Statenborough House in Kent, and the family also had links with the old city of Rochester in Kent. Both names were to be given to streets in the Adelaide subdivision.[13]

The relationship between the Osborns and the Mouldens went back to Joseph's football days in the mid 1870s when they were business associates and friends. The Mouldens acted as solicitors for the Osborns at an early stage, and still do. Bayfield Moulden's 'handsome villa', surrounded by a four-acre reserve, was located next to the Osborns', between Rochester and Statenborough streets.

The Osborn property is described as one of 'four imposing residences' in Elizabeth Warburton's *The Paddocks Beneath: A History of Burnside from the Beginning*:

> *The fourth of these Glynburn Road villas was built in 1883 by Joseph Rowe*
> *Osborn (1852‑1921). It is an attractive single-storeyed bluestone house whose*
> *original setting of trees, orange grove, gardens and lawns that swept down*
> *to Second Creek must have made it a sight to behold. Even now, numbered*
> *39 Rochester Street, its trees and lawn protect it gracefully from heat and noise.*[14]

Joseph Osborn purchased his land from the Mouldens. As a successful racehorse owner, he no doubt financed the property through his winnings. Between 1895 and 1913 Osborn amassed 72 wins, earning stake money of £19271. He was high on the list of winning owners in South Australia; in the years 1900–01, 1902–03, 1904–05 and 1905–06 he held first position.[15] He also speculated in mining shares. On 4 February 1886 he bought five shares in the Broken Hill Proprietary Company, which had formed on 13 August 1885. At that time the face value of the shares was £20, and they were quoted on the Adelaide Stock Exchange at up to £26. Whether he paid £20 or £26, this was a substantial investment at the time. By March 1888 Osborn had acquired more shares, and on 6 March 1888 he transferred 20 shares to his wife. At that date they were being quoted at £360 to £373, a remarkable increase in investment over two years. A few weeks later, on 15 April 1888, Mary Jane gave birth to a son, Francis Ernest. The transfer of shares may have been in recognition of the forthcoming happy event.[16] The family cannot explain why Joseph and Mary named their home 'Rochdale'. Rochdale is a large city in Lancashire, England,

north of Manchester, yet there is no evidence that either had any connection with the place. Perhaps it was so named simply because it was located in Rochester Street.

In the first decade of the twentieth century the two Osborn daughters, Mary and Edith, were married. Mary Elizabeth, born 21 April 1884, married James (Jim) Allan Carlyle Marshall in 1909. Jim was a director of James Marshall & Company, a firm of drapers in Rundle Street founded by his father, also James Marshall. After their marriage the Marshalls lived across Glynburn Road from the Osborns for some years before moving to 'Darroch', a large Victorian villa in Payneham Road that had been owned by the first James Marshall.[17]

Joseph and Mary's youngest daughter, Edith Florence, born 21 February 1891, married Theo Felstead on 16 December 1914 at the Marshalls' residence in Burnside. Theo, the fifth son of William Henry Felstead and Sara (née Ormond), was born in St Kilda, Victoria, in 1891. He attended Haylebury College in Melbourne then Roseworthy College in South Australia. The couple probably met through mutual acquaintances. Theo and Edith had one son, John Rowe Felstead. In 1916 Theo enlisted in Melbourne in the 1st Australian Squadron of the Australian Imperial Force as a second lieutenant. He died at the Kooyong Road Military Hospital, Caulfield, of nephrotomy and heart failure on 16 January 1918, aged 24 years. Two years after Theo's death, Edith married Samuel (Sam) Elderton Tolley on 24 November 1920 at St Peter's College Chapel. Sam was by then managing director of Tolley, Scott & Tolley, wine and brandy makers. The couple then lived at Railway Terrace, Nuriootpa; they had no children. Sam had served with Edith's brother, Frank, in the 43rd Battalion AIF and had been best man at Frank's wedding to Helena d'Arenberg in June 1920.[18]

After Joseph Osborn's death on 25 May 1921, Mary and her unmarried sister Robina Stewart continued to live at 'Rochdale'. In 1924 they moved to a house Mary had built on land opposite 'Darroch', where her daughter and son-in-law lived. She often provided accommodation for her grandchildren as they grew to adulthood, and this became an Osborn family tradition. John Felstead lived with Granny Osborn before he joined the RAAF, Toni when she was in the Women's Australian National Service, and Rowen during his last three years of school and also while at university in Adelaide. She remained in the house opposite 'Darroch' until her death in March 1957.

Frank Osborn: from 'useful change bowler' to 'vigneron'

Joseph and Mary's second son, and third child, Francis Ernest (Frank), was born on 15 April 1888. When he arrived in McLaren Vale in his early twenties, Frank was a man of average height with hazel eyes and dark hair. A photograph of him playing for the Adelaide University intervarsity cricket team in 1910 portrays him as a serious young man — but to him, cricket was a serious business. Other photographs of him in a social context reveal a spectacled young man with a tentative smile.

Frank and his brother and sisters grew up at 'Rochdale', 39 Rochester Street. His first school, Knightsbridge School at 28 Statenborough Street, run by Mrs Edith Hubbe and her sister Miss Harriet Cook, took students from kindergarten to university entrance. Frank spent six years there then went to Canterbury School in Kent Town. Canterbury was opened in October 1899; its headmaster was the well-known Reverend Frederic Slaney-Poole, MA.[19] Slaney-Poole had arrived in South Australia from England in 1867. He had served in a number of South Australian parishes in Adelaide and Ballarat, Victoria, and had also lectured in Classics at the University of Adelaide from 1878 to 1895. Frank was enrolled at Canterbury School from 1900; in 1902 he won the Holy Scripture Prize and in 1903 he collected a prize 'For Year's Marks'.[20] In February 1904 Frank moved to Prince Alfred College (PAC), Kent Town; he was almost 16 years of age and began in the fifth form.

The love of the game

Frank's academic progress at PAC seems to have been unexceptional, although he passed the Senior Public Examination in 1907 and so gained university entrance.[21] However, as befitting the son of Joseph Osborn, he was a keen participant in other school activities, especially sport. In the third term of 1904 the school magazine, the *Prince Alfred College Chronicle*, described him as 'a useful change bowler'. In the summer of 1904–05, he was briefly demoted to the seconds but finished the cricket season with the firsts.[22]

In 1905 he competed against Wesley College football team who were visiting from Melbourne. In the winter of 1906 Frank was prominent in school football. A visiting side from Scotch College, Melbourne, defeated PAC, but the *Chronicle* noted that Osborn was 'sure in goal and kicked off well'. In July 1906 spectators saw St Peter's defeat PAC by 14–14 to 6–6 at the Adelaide oval. Frank played well in a busy time as fullback, the *Chronicle* describing some of his high kicks as 'exalted'. In 1906 he was in the team when St Peter's beat Prince Alfred College in a boarders' intercollegiate sports day.

Frank's style at the Annual Cricket Match, Red vs Blue, on Saturday, 8 December 1906, once again caught the attention of the *Chronicle* reporter, this time in a positive way. In assessing each of the players, 'Osborn, F E' is described as:

Very good bat, with strokes all round the wicket; rather too fond, however, of hooking and getting his leg in front of the wicket; fast bowler, keeps a good length and uses his head well; poor in the field owing to nervousness.[23]

Nervousness was not a quality the family associated with him in later life. In 1906 he competed in intercollegiate gymnastics and in a team of 12 who took part in the club swimming competition. Frank used to tell his children that he won a chest-expansion competition in an intercol, but they later suspected he was pulling their leg. By 1907, as befitted a senior boy (he was then 19 years of age), Frank was a power in the school's sporting activities, serving on the general sports, cricket, tennis, football and swimming committees. He travelled to Melbourne in August 1907 to play against Scotch and Wesley colleges. Both games were lost but he was prominent in the game against Scotch. *The Scotch Collegian* noted that 'Willsmore, Steele, Osborn, Graves, Matters, Cooper and Randell played finely'.[24] In the Wesley game, he left the field because of injury. In the intercollegiate cricket in

December 1907, Frank's performance was reported again in the *Chronicle*. In the early part of the game he was 'given out as having just touched the first ball of the day'.[25] Later, however:

> *F E Osborn — fastest bowler in the team; his off-theory is of good length and very accurate and he varies his pace well; forcible bat, and scores quickly; greatly missed in the match against the Saints.*[26]

In response to patriotic sentiments aroused by the Boer War, in 1900 a cadet corps was established at Prince Alfred. In 1905 about 100 boys, including Frank, joined the corps. He became one of four sergeants in the two companies. In May 1906 the *Chronicle* reported that the Cadet Corps '[met] every Wednesday and under Sergeant Osborn…were undergoing vigorous training'. Later in the year the *Chronicle* reported that the corps had a strength of 157 in three companies and 'Osborn was among those at once recommended for commission, on the strength of their work as sergeants in 1905'. He resigned his commission in May 1908 when he left the school. Although he passed the Senior Public Examination in 1907, Frank was back at school at the beginning of 1908, when he was made joint secretary of the sports committee. However, school records indicate he left in May of that year to begin the first year of the MBBS course at the University of Adelaide. It is puzzling that he re-enrolled at PAC at the beginning of the year when he began his medical degree a month later. Either a place in medicine was not guaranteed or available until the last moment, or he simply wanted to continue playing sport at PAC. More puzzling is the fact that at the end of that year he received the 'Senior Prize V1c Form'. The bookplate on his prize, G A Henty's *For Name and Fame*, is dated 'Christmas 1908'.

Frank's name appears on the list of students enrolled at Adelaide University in the MBBS degree in 1908, 1909 and 1910. Clearly his heart was not in his studies: he did not make the pass list in any year. His sister Edith spoke of bad health having affected his performance in at least one of the years. He was ill, and injured, as a result of a trial with his father's old football club, Norwood. He told his sons that, at his first training run at Norwood, two of the players decided to toughen up the schoolboy recruit and 'sandwiched' him. He suffered a crushed chest, developed pneumonia and did not try out again with the club. It is possible that this prank was the root cause of the poor health that would plague him for much of his life.

Yet football remained Frank's abiding passion. Once they reached university, a number of former PAC students who had played cricket and football with Frank decided to enter the university football team. The team was not popular with the South Australian Football League, however. The university's application for inclusion in the league had been denied twice on the grounds that it would break up the 'electorate' system. The Adelaide *Advertiser* recognised that all 'A' grade football teams (except Port Adelaide) would lose players to the university if it was admitted to the league. The paper included Frank Osborn among potential players not already playing with one of the league clubs. The only reference to Frank's playing football after leaving PAC is the inclusion of an 'Osborne' in the Old Scholars team that played the school at the Adelaide Oval on 7 July 1909. The school won by 15 goals 8 behinds to 6 goals 11 behinds.

The summer of 1908–09 saw Adelaide University admitted to the 'A' grade district cricket competition for the first time. Frank made his debut in the team's second match on Saturday, 21 November, going in at number 10 and being bowled for just one run.[27] This was the start of an undistinguished season, but he held his place in the side. His best score was 37, against Glenelg, although the return game against Adelaide on 20 March 1909 led the *Advertiser* to comment, 'Osborn batted vigorously for 19. He appears to have the makings of a fine bat. He has confidence and shapes attractively'.

In the 1909–10 season Frank began with the University 'B' team; his performance of clean bowling four and finishing 5 for 13 gained him a place in the 'A' team for the rest of the season. In the first half of the 1910–11 season he played 'A' grade once again, but in one game was out for a duck. The Adelaide *Advertiser* thought poorly of the decision, which in the minds of many of the onlookers was open to doubt. He played two more games before the end of the year, without success or distinction. He was included in the Adelaide University XI that visited Melbourne and played on 24 December 1910. This was probably the first Christmas he spent away from his family. It was also the first match between the two university elevens, the *Sydney Morning Herald* describing it as an inter-university test. The match, which was not restricted to undergraduates as Adelaide were not able to field a compact eleven of undergraduates, was won by Sydney. Adelaide made 317 in their first innings (Osborn lbw) and were dismissed for only 129 in the second (Frank scored only 4). Sydney made 295 in their first innings (Osborn 2 for 58) and 356 for 4 in their second, winning by six wickets.

A false start

Frank maintained his interest in his old school; he was elected a member of the committee of the Prince Alfred Old Collegians Association at its annual general meeting in September 1910. Like his father, Frank was more sportsman than scholar. He failed his university examinations in Adelaide at the end of 1910. Hoping to achieve distinction elsewhere, he enrolled at the University of Melbourne on 3 March 1911, having been accepted for First Year Medicine. He found a place at Ormond College. On Saturday, 11 March, the Adelaide *Advertiser* noted his departure:

> *Mr Frank Osborne who was a passenger to Melbourne, where he intends continuing his medical studies, was tendered a farewell by the Committee of the Prince Alfred Old Collegians Association at the South Australian Hotel on Friday afternoon.*[28]

At the University of Melbourne he enrolled in Natural Philosophy 1, Chemistry 1, Biology 1 and Elementary Anatomy. However, Frank's move to Melbourne failed to bring success to his studies. In November 1911 he failed his first three subjects and did not sit for the fourth.

Despite his love of the game, Frank found it hard to break into the Ormond College football team — it was 'rather a closed shop', he said later. That was a fair comment. The University of Melbourne was an élite institution, attended overwhelmingly by the wealthier class. Scholarships were limited to 40 per year. Frank had to contend with being something of an outsider in Melbourne and one who enjoyed sport more than study, although he would not have been alone in that.[29] However, the concept of the University of Melbourne as a 'closed shop' was not new — it had always been thus. Indeed, until the 1960s the university was known as 'the Shop' for slightly different reasons from those Frank might have imagined. It was seen merely as a degree-producing factory where select individuals could attend, study a little and collect a degree at the end of the required time. It was, in subtle ways, 'closed' to outsiders.[30]

Onto the land

While in Melbourne, Frank frequently visited the family of Frederick and Georgina Heath at 'Bundarra', 666 Toorak Road, Toorak; the family had South Australian connections. Frank's sister Mary had often visited their Melbourne home before her marriage. Frederick William Heath was a director of Thomas Gaunt, Jewellers, of Melbourne. The firm, among other things, supplied chronometers to the Victorian Racing Club. The family think Frank's father knew Heath through his racing interests and his membership of the committee of the Adelaide Racing Club. The Heaths were one of Melbourne's well-connected and long-established families. Their daughter Dorothy married Harold Darling, a contemporary of James Marshall at Prince Alfred College in Adelaide in the 1890s, hence the Adelaide connection. From 1936 to 1950 Darling was a director of the Broken Hill Pty Co. Their daughter Elizabeth Darling married John Madden Baillieu, partner of E L and C Baillieu Stockbroking Ltd and grandson of William Lawrence Baillieu.

What did Joseph and Mary say to Frank when he returned from Melbourne in 1911? He had failed his medical courses at both Adelaide and Melbourne universities. This meant his parents' ambitions for him to become a doctor remained unfulfilled. Anecdotal evidence suggests Frank expressed a hope of going onto the land. It is highly likely that Tom Nottage, a nephew of Thomas Hardy and family friend, suggested that the Milton property, then on the market, would be an ideal buy for the Osborns.[31]

On 4 December 1911 Joseph Osborn paid a deposit of £3600 for the option to buy the Milton property, which was made up of Sections 108 and 118, Hundred of Willunga. The sale was to be concluded by 2 April 1912. It was exercised by the further payment of £20 400 and on 10 April 1912 Sections 108 and 118 were transferred from T S Milton, L A Milton and Alice Rayner (née Milton) to Joseph Rowe Osborn of Adelaide, merchant, and Francis Ernest Osborn of McLaren Vale, vigneron, as joint tenants. Frank called his new property Bundarra Vineyards in the belief that *bundarra* was an Aboriginal word meaning 'on a hill'. Of course, it was also the name of the home owned by their family friends the Heaths in Melbourne. Initially Frank was unaware that a vineyard of that name, established by Richard Bailey in the 1870s, already existed near Glenrowan in the north-west of Victoria. It was decades after Frank named his vineyard that the Baileys of Glenrowan claimed copyright on the name.

Speaking with Rowen Osborn in 1975, two of Tom Milton's daughters, Winifred Muirhead and Elma Renfrey, remembered Frank Osborn and his brother-in-law James Marshall inspecting the property before Frank and his father agreed to purchase it.[32] Frank's first few years on the land were spent learning all he could about grape growing, wine and winemaking. Naturally, he also seized the opportunity to play for the McLaren Vale cricket team in the 1912–13 season.

When he first established himself in the Vale, Frank bought a pair of grey horses and a four-wheeled, American-style buggy; he was very proud of this acquisition. But in early 1913, not to be outdone by his neighbour Frederick Shipster, the owner of the first motorcar in McLaren Vale, Frank bought an impressive car. It was the very popular De Dion, and family records reveal that he proudly made his final payment of £289 16s 6d on 30 June that year, only months after he purchased it. And so began a lifelong passion for cars.

Army service

Frank enlisted in the Australian Imperial Force on 2 August 1915, four months after the disaster at Gallipoli in April 1915. On 21 August an oak tree was planted at the McLaren Vale Recreation Ground for each of the men and a silver birch for each of the nurses who had enlisted. The Adelaide *Advertiser* reported on 25 August 1915 that the McLaren Vale district had 'furnished quite a number of volunteers for active service at the front, namely, three nurses, one chaplain and 27 soldiers'.[33] The soldiers included F E Osborn.

Frank was certified as fit and reported to the Base Infantry Depot at Mitcham one week after enlisting, on 9 August 1915. While his boyhood health problems with rheumatism would return before long, for the moment he was happy and proud to have enlisted. His recurring ill health meant that of the 311 days between his enlistment in August 1915 and his departure for England with his battalion in June 1916, he was sick with rheumatism and tonsilitis for 31 days. From 1 September to 15 October 1915 Frank attended Non-Commissioned Officers (NCO) School and was promoted to sergeant. For the next three months he attended Officers' Training School and on 20 January 1916 received his commission as second lieutenant.[34] He was transferred, along with 31 other officers, to the newly formed 43rd Battalion, 3rd Division, AIF.[35]

Frank's experience in the battalion camped at Morphettville racecourse was less triumphant than his father's racing successes there. On 3 May 1916 the battalion was ordered to 'march out' of the camp and through Adelaide before marching back to camp on 9 May — an indicator, perhaps, of future combat experience? On Friday, 9 June, the battalion travelled by train to Outer Harbour, where the SS *Afric* awaited the troops and 'a large and enthusiastic crowd' bade them farewell.[36] The battalion historians record that:

> *Never in the history of the State had so large a crowd assembled to witness the departure of a boat. Hundreds of coloured streamers soon linked up the soldiers on board with the crowd on the wharf, the intermingling of colour presenting a spectacle long to remain in the memories of those present.*[37]

No doubt Frank's family were on the wharf, watching and waving, when the SS *Afric* departed at 2.00 pm that Friday afternoon. They sailed via Albany, Western Australia, and Colombo to the Mediterranean, where the Royal Navy provided an escort through the Mediterranean to Marseilles. On 19 July the company

disembarked and boarded a train to Le Havre, Normandy. On the way they stopped at Avignon and passed through Lyons and Dijon where, Frank recorded later, the French Red Cross served tea and cakes, then on through Juvisy, Versailles, the Seine Valley and Nantes to Le Havre, where they spent a cold night. The 43rd Battalion was bound for England and on 23 July they crossed the Channel on the *Duke of Connaught*, arriving at Southampton the next morning. From there they travelled to Lark Hill on the Salisbury Plain, where they joined the 41st, 42nd and 44th battalions of 11th Brigade. Additional training began, with some officers and NCOs sent to military schools for specialised instruction. Frank's ill health persisted throughout his enlistment. His training while he was unwell included a musketry course at Hayling Island.

On 25 November 1916 the battalion departed for Southampton and shipped back to Le Havre then travelled by troop train to St Omer, near Calais; they were billeted in farmhouses and barns while training continued. Frank was promoted to first lieutenant on 1 December 1916. The 11th Brigade were to take over responsibility for 'the line' with the 43rd and 44th supporting the 41st and 42nd battalions, who were holding the battle line. On the night of 29–30 December the battalion relieved the 41st in the line, and until March 1917 the 41st and 43rd alternated in the trenches every six days.

Frank's health, already poor, was aggravated by the cold, wet weather and the appalling conditions. On 3 January 1917 he was evacuated and on 7 January he was admitted to the 14th General Hospital at Boulogne, where he was diagnosed with myositis, a disease causing muscular inflammation. Shipped back to London, on 13 January he was admitted to the 3rd London General Hospital, Wandsworth, and diagnosed with rheumatism. He remained in London for six months. On 22 July 1917 Frank left England on the *Nestor*, arriving in Adelaide, to the delight of his family, on 21 September. He was discharged on 9 November 1917. His final medical condition was described as myalgia (muscular) rheumatism and sciatica. Before his discharge an Australian Military Forces Medical Board found that he suffered from persistent rheumatism aggravated by active service and that he was unfit for service either at home or abroad.

When he arrived home 'Rochdale' and other houses in the street were decorated with streamers in his honour. To assist his convalescence, Frank spent some time on Todmorden Station, about 35 miles north of Oodnadatta, itself 700 miles north of Adelaide, where it was thought the hot, dry climate might relieve his rheumatism. His personal reflections of his time in Todmorden have been lost, but his collection of Aboriginal boomerangs, killing-sticks, a bull-roarer, strings of beads and other artefacts surely set him apart from most men of his time. He later displayed these artefacts at his McLaren Vale home.

Frank had had only three short years to enjoy life on the land before enlisting in the Great War, but persistent poor health had cut short his service career. Now recuperated and back at Bundarra, Frank could pour all his energies and passion into the vineyard. It was time for Frank to become a 'vigneron'.

CHAPTER 2

Bundarra Vineyards — the beginnings

JOHN REYNELL, ONE OF THE FIRST SETTLERS IN THE McLAREN VALE REGION, laid the foundations of his vineyard and winery, Reynella, in 1838. George Manning's Hope Farm was planted in 1850.[1] In 1854 Thomas Hardy started growing Shiraz and Grenache vines in the region. The other significant contributor to the early years of winemaking in McLaren Vale was Dr Alexander Kelly who, with four others, formed The Tintara Vineyard Company in 1862. Fifteen years later Hardy salvaged the bankrupt Tintara Vineyards, bought the old McLaren Vale flourmill and converted it into a winery. By the late 1880s Thomas Hardy had convinced a number of local farmers to shift from farming to grape growing. Several more pioneering vineyards and cellars were established by the turn of the century. These included Tatachilla Vineyard (1887–88), Kay Brothers' Amery Vineyard (1890) and the Johnston family's Pirramimma (1891). Other ventures included Frank Wilkinson's Ryecroft (1895), Pridmore's The Wattles (1896) and, in 1900, Katunga and Wirra Wirra. By the early 1900s there were 19 wineries in the district. McLaren Vale soon became a major winemaking region of South Australia, producing full-bodied red wine and port; the major market for the wine was the United Kingdom. The history of the Osborn vineyards, and later d'Arenberg Wines, begins only 13 years after South Australia won statehood.

Bundarra, 1912

The property the Osborns bought from Tom Milton and his family consisted of 195 acres — two sections of 80 acres each, one of 33 acres and a former road of 2 acres. It included a four-room stone house with front and back verandahs, a semi-underground dairy, a stone-walled stable for six horses and a two-bale milking shed with thatched roof and slab sides. Frank's first job was to replace the cottage's compacted dirt floors with timber and to build two rooms onto the western side of the cottage for his own use. His second job was to hire Spencer Norman (Norm) King and his wife, Mary, for farm, vineyard and domestic duties. The original homestead building was extended again in 1996 and now houses the restaurant d'Arry's Verandah. The various sections of land have interesting stories of their own.

Sections 108 and 118

The Osborns are the fourth owners of their land. They were preceded by Jonathan and Ann Barrans and their children, another farming family, the Pavys, and finally the farmer turned vigneron William Milton and his family.

On 14 September 1849 Sections 108 and 118 were granted to Jonathan Barrans of Mitcham for £80 each.[2] He was also granted Section 740, for which he paid £80 1s 0d. The land grants were issued by the Lieutenant-Governor, Sir Henry Young. The land grant documents bear the signature and seal of both the Lieutenant-Governor and Charles Sturt, the Colonial Secretary.[3]

Jonathan Barrans was a 'currier' — that is, a dresser and dyer of leather after it is tanned. Although the year of his birth and arrival in South Australia are uncertain,[4] it is known that he was a Corps Major in the 2nd Life Guards in 1839 and that the family was active in Mitcham for many years.[5] Barrans died in November 1861. His wife, Ann, who died on 9 March 1878 in her sixty-ninth year, was listed as a vigneron in Boothby's *Adelaide Almanac and Directory*. Both are buried in the Mitcham cemetery. The land, it appears, was destined to produce wine.

Barrans' will provided for 'life estate' in his property at McLaren Vale to pass to his widow and then to George Prince and Jonathan Robert Walker in trust to dispose of as they saw fit. Walker died on 20 March 1876, so when Ann Barrans died the property passed to the surviving Executor and Trustee, George Prince. Walker's occupation is unknown, but Prince is listed in the *Biographical Index of South Australia* as, variously, the Reverend George Prince, a warehouseman and an agriculturalist. A man of many talents.

Prince wasted no time: he sold the three sections (108, 118 and 740) on 1 July 1878 to Joseph Holmes Barrans, one of Jonathan and Ann's sons, for £780. Joseph himself held the land for only one month before selling it to William Henry Hammond, gentleman, on 1 August 1878 for £820, also making a minor but quick capital gain. When Hammond died at McLaren Vale on 20 November 1890 his estate passed to four women, Lydia Pavy, Eliza Hillyer, Catherine Webber (née Hammond) and Caroline Hammond (née Webber), The women's relationship to William Hammond and to each other is unclear. A Certificate of Title[6] was issued only to William Pavy, husband of Lydia Pavy, on 7 March 1891. Then on 1 April 1891 William Pavy sold Sections 108 and

118 to the farmer William Milton. The first 55 acres of vines planted by Milton were part of the 1890s expansion of viticulture in the McLaren Vale instigated and encouraged by Thomas Hardy.[7]

William Milton held the property from 1891 until his death on 2 January 1905. His son, Tom Steven Milton (1866–1947), was his executor and became a proprietor of Sections 108 and 118.[8] On 3 June 1908 Lewin Allan Milton, vigneron, of McLaren Vale, and Alice Rose Edith Rayner, wife of Edward Rayner of McLaren Vale, joined Tom Milton as owners of the property. The extended Milton family finalised the sale of the property to Joseph Rowe Osborn and his son Frank on 10 April 1912. The Osborns paid £24000 for Sections 108 and 118. Section 740 remained with the Pavy family and never became part of Osborn Vineyards.

Section 740

Subsequent sales of the Pavys' property, Section 740, began in 1891. William Pavy sold Section 740 on 25 March 1891 to the accountant Herbert Kay of Adelaide, and on 28 May 1892 Frederick Walter Kay joined his brother Herbert as joint owner of that section. This was the location of the Kay family's Amery Vineyard and the brothers both gave their address as Amery, McLaren Vale, their occupations as vignerons. Years later the Kay brothers told Frank Osborn that they had considered buying Sections 108 and 118 but were looking for bigger acreage, possibly on the one block since they established their enterprise on Section 740 and three adjoining sections, 514, 515 and 516.

Section 128

Section 128 was originally granted to Archibald Boyd, Esquire, of Kilburgh, Scotland, for £80 on 13 July 1857.[9] It was a speculator's dream. On 13 August 1857 Boyd sold Section 128 to Parkin Lumb, 'of Tanunga near McLaren Vale', for £500.[10] Lumb lived on Section 126, and may also have owned Sections 127, 116 and 117. He built his cottage on Section 126, just above the floor of a little valley; it survived until after the Second World War.[11] Lumb was one of the original five councillors of the Noarlunga District Council, proclaimed in August 1856.

On 19 August 1857, the day after he bought Section 128 from Boyd, Lumb mortgaged the property to Adolphus William Young for £250 plus interest. The mortgage was extended but on 26 March 1869 Lumb sold it to Walter Dunstan for the £350 remaining on the mortgage. Young called in the mortgage but Dunstan, being unable to discharge it, then sold the section to Young on 27 October 1870.[12] How the Englishman Adolphus Young came to invest in land in McLaren Vale is something of a mystery. He originally settled in New South Wales but found earning a living a little trying, so possibly he bought the land as a speculator. He soon returned to England, however, where he inherited 'Hare Hatch House' in Berkshire from his father. He died there on 4 November 1885, leaving an estate of some £27 000 to his widow and eight surviving children.[13]

Eight years after Young's death, in February 1893 Section 128 was sold back to Parkin Lumb, who then mortgaged it to James Edward Day and later also to Josiah Henry Symon. These mortgages were discharged on 28 March 1900 when Lumb sold the section to Henry Frederick Shipster, a mysterious character who described himself as a man 'of parts beyond the seas, gentlemen'. Shipster was born around 1842 and arrived in South Australia with his father, George Frederick Shipster, and his family on the *Madras*. His father, a solicitor who died on 30 December 1844, had been interested in South Australia, having bought Town Acre 125, Adelaide, in 1837 while still in England. An early McLaren Vale settler, James Sykes, is said by G H Manning in *Hope Farm: Cradle of McLaren Vale Wine Industry* to have bought Sections 116, 117 and 138 from Henry Shipster in March 1865 for £1050.[14] If Lumb in fact owned Sections 116 and 117 in 1882, he presumably bought them from Sykes, who, according to Manning, had them heavily mortgaged.

Henry Shipster married Eliza Younghusband, daughter of an early Premier of South Australia, William Younghusband, on 12 September 1864. They had a son, Frederick Palmer Shipster, to whom Henry transferred Section 128 (and doubtless other nearby sections) on 14 July 1904. Frederick Palmer Shipster was then described as a vigneron at McLaren Vale and may have been living on the property. Frederick Palmer Shipster is another character whose story will never be fully known.

Further transactions on the land took place. In September 1916 Shipster transferred Section 128 to Reginald Nash Spong, a pastoralist in Northern Australia, who transferred it to his son of the same name, known as Rex, on 24 April 1946. Rex later subdivided the section along a natural watercourse, selling the northern 33 acres, more or less, to the Osborn family in November 1958 for £4000. This portion had been planted with vines and a small orchard of prunus and included an avenue of pines planted by Frederick Shipster.

The purchase of the northern portion of Section 128 (Spong's land) in 1958 completed the Osborn property, then called Osborn Vineyards. Over almost 150 years the three pieces of land involved have passed through a variety of hands including an ex-army officer, tanner, wool sorter, preacher, investor, lawyer, merchant, timber merchant and member of the House of Commons, as well as farmers and vignerons.

Old vines in the new world

The Milton property, as purchased, was planted with 33 acres of Shiraz, 16 acres of Mataro and 4 acres of currants. Joseph and Frank knew that the Miltons had been planning further plantings before the sale. The anticipated yield for 1911 was calculated to be:

33 ACRES SHIRAZ	99 TONS	£500
4 ACRES CURRANTS	5 TONS	£160
16 ACRES MATARO	40 TONS	£200
TOTAL	144 TONS	£860

In 1911 the 15 acres under crop were expected to yield 27 bushels of grain per acre as well as an unspecified amount of 'trombones, potatoes, etc.'.

The first plantings

In 1912 the first new vines planted by Frank Osborn were Shiraz grapes; he planted eight acres on the south-east corner of Section 118 bordering on Twenty Eight Road. Only about four of the acres planted survived, the more exposed portion of ground reverting to light scrub regrowth. Frank also planted a few rows of Shiraz at the top of a Milton planted block known as the 'Side of the Hill' because it was on the eastern hill forming the smaller valley running south in the centre of Section 118. Verna Jacobs, one of Tom Milton's daughters, recalled in 1989 that Frank Osborn's first vintage, 1913, totalled 100 tonnes and that the grapes reached the 'unheard of' price of £20 per tonne.[15]

The three existing varieties of grapes — Shiraz, Mataro and currants — originally planted by the Miltons, were typical of vines planted in the McLaren Vale in the 1890s. Shiraz or Syrah, indigenous to the northern Rhône in France, has been described as 'an excellent grape … A very hardy plant [that] produces very well, and seems to be liable to no accident or disease'.[16] It is as well suited to making tawny and vintage port as it is to table wine. The Mataro grape was the dominant grape variety in Provence until the phylloxera outbreak of the 1870s. It produces a wine high in alcohol and tannins that make it ideal as a blending variety. As James Halliday notes, the main producers of Mataro (also known as Mourvèdre) are the McLaren Vale and the Barossa Valley. d'Arenberg is known as one of South Australia's best producers of Mourvèdre.[17] The first currants planted in the McLaren Vale in 1878 by Thomas Hardy bore no fruit. Later, cuttings of the Zante currant were first trialled by Hardy at his Bankside vineyard. He then introduced them into McLaren

Vale, grafting them on to Grenache vines.[18] Often integrated with wine grapes, currants remained a major source of income for farmers in the McLaren Vale until the 1940s and at d'Arenberg until the late 1950s.

In his first years as a vigneron, Frank Osborn's Shiraz and Mataro grapes were sold to the large McLaren Vale producers for export. McLaren Vale became a 'stronghold' of Shiraz grapes and, through the Emu Wine Company, specialised in the export of Shiraz to the United Kingdom.[19] The Shiraz wine from the Osborn vineyard has been described as 'ferruginous'. This term was used to describe the Shiraz exported to the United Kingdom, accompanied by advertisements of white-haired doctors recommending to frail old ladies 'ferruginous flagons' of 'Australian Burgundy' as a tonic.[20]

Echoes of war

Drought and the outbreak of war in 1914, followed by Frank's enlistment in August 1915, curtailed plans for further development and planting at Bundarra. In Frank's absence, work in the vineyard was probably supervised by Jim Marshall or Norm King. It is assumed that Joseph advised from a distance: records have not survived to confirm this. In the summer of 1916, when Frank received his commission, the state was experiencing a very severe heat wave. Although South Australia was spared scorching winds, the Shiraz grapes were forced forward to such a degree that those grown on limestone ridges had to be harvested immediately to prevent losses. The grapes, it appears, did not suffer from a complete lack of rain during the summer, and it was anticipated that the crop would weigh better than any for the past two years.[21]

As worrying as the weather was to the wine industry, winemaker Oscar Seppelt bemoaned the fact that it was impossible for 'the Australian vigneron to benefit by the present remarkable demand' for wine. As well as the weather, the price of grapes had risen sharply, wages, freight and the price of casks had gone up and 'every other commodity used by the vignerons had to be paid for at enhanced rates'.[22] In short, the winemaker had to pass on the additional costs to the consumer. Seppelt concluded that the liquor business was passing through a 'most trying phase of its existence' and those who had invested their money in the industry dreaded what the future might hold for them. Assuming he read the wine industry journal, we wonder how Joseph took this dour warning.

In Frank's absence in 1916, Jim Marshall oversaw the planting of an additional 32 acres of Shiraz and Grenache vines, 'the world's most planted red variety'.[23] It was the first year to record the planting of Grenache vines at Bundarra; by 1928 they had a total of 12 acres. James Halliday informs us that both Spain and Sardinia claim Grenache as their own. It was in cultivation by the beginning of the fourteenth century; its cultivation then spread outwards from Aragon across northern Spain and southern France. In the New World it was embraced in California and South Australia, establishing itself in the warmest, driest areas of those regions. In Australia, Grenache thrives particularly well in the McLaren Vale. Encouraged by Thomas Hardy, the main varieties of Shiraz, Mataro and Grenache first planted in the district were also planted by the Miltons and later the Osborns for sale to Hardy's, either for export or to be made into port.

The Great War initially had little effect on Australian wine exports to the United Kingdom; in fact, 1915 exports reached the highest volume since 1911.[24] However, when German submarine activity increased and Allied shipping resources were reserved for vital supplies, a drop in exports inevitably followed: from 503 445 gallons in 1916 to 289 518 in 1917, then to 176 029 gallons in 1918. A contributing factor was the Anglo-Portuguese Treaty of 1916, which gave Portugal the exclusive use of the terms 'port' and 'madeira' in the British market. Australia winemakers were compelled to describe their port as 'port type', implying that it was not 'real' port. Australian exporters competed unequally with Portugal, which had freight advantages; both wines paid the same duty.

Building Bundarra

In 1919, with his health improved and his betrothal to Helena d'Arenberg announced, Frank Osborn engaged Monty Jackman of Jackman & Treloar Architects to design a bungalow-style house at McLaren Vale. Set to the east of the original cottage, it was completed in 1920 at a cost of £1400. With its red-tiled roof and brick walls on ironstone foundations, and stuccoed white, it could be seen from afar. For years it was one of only two tile-roofed houses in the area. Helen no doubt had a hand in the planning. When teased by her friends about leaving the city for the rigours of country life, she enjoyed painting a false picture of how uncomfortable living would be. When her friends visited her there, some were surprised to find the bathroom contained the latest technology — an inside toilet

serviced by a septic tank. She probably enjoyed leading them on.

Approached from the south, the house has a front verandah leading to a porch and the front door, with another long verandah on the west side. It includes a hall, a sitting room separated from the dining room by panelling and glass doors, a pantry, a servery, a kitchen, two bedrooms, one bathroom and a cellar under the kitchen. Massive ironstone-faced fireplaces dominate the sitting and dining rooms; each bedroom has a fireplace and a handbasin. A laundry was originally attached to the north-east corner of the house. The western wall of the sitting room had a picture window; and a door with small lead-framed glass window panels in the adjoining dining room wall opened onto the verandah. Superb views to the south stretching across to McLaren Vale two miles away to the Willunga Hills and away to the south-east to Gulf St Vincent and Cape Jervois, some 35 miles further, could be enjoyed only from the two bedrooms, not from the sitting room where two small windows high on the south wall flanked the fireplace and chimney breast. The family speculate that the house was incorrectly positioned when the foundations were laid, and that the picture window in the sitting room was meant to face south with a view to the landscape. Frank was holidaying on Kangaroo Island at Jim Marshall's shack when the foundations for the house were laid, which meant he was unable to oversee the placement of the building.

A reliable water supply was essential. The Miltons had tried to sink a well below the old cottage. Robert Oliver, whose family owned the adjoining property on the western side, sank a shaft but no water was found and the shaft was eventually filled in. Before Frank Osborn arrived a windmill had been erected on a well near the boundary with the Olivers' property (west of the cottage), and a tank and a trough were installed. A small dam had also been dug just below the stables in what was known as the Dam Paddock. The supply from this well also proved unsatisfactory — the wind never seemed to blow when water was needed — so Frank sought a site for a bore with an engine-driven pump. Excellent water was found in a gully on the north side near Twenty Eight Road, the eastern boundary of the property. Power was supplied by a Fuller Johnson engine and water pumped to a 20 000-gallon 'squatter's tank' on the ground between the cottage and the new house.[25] Construction of the house included a 32-volt electric light from a Delco generator. Water from the tank was connected to the garden at the cottage, although their neighbours the Kings mostly relied on rainwater tanks. Two steel tank stands were built beside the main tank and water was pumped from it into stand tanks that supplied the house and then the winery.

At this stage the vineyard boasted three currant-drying sheds to the north of the new house. Rainwater collected from their roofs was piped into the kitchen of the house. A 6000-gallon semi-underground tank and three galvanised iron tanks provided additional rainwater storage; water is still pumped from the 6000-gallon tank to a tank above the ceiling of the house to provide pressure for domestic supply. Within a few years sand blocked the bore near Twenty Eight Road, and in 1928 a new bore was sunk in the valley below the house on the southern side. A Petter Junior engine pumped water to the tanks near the house. For years the bore yielded about 480 gallons an hour, subject to occasional interruptions caused by breakdowns. Eventually sand blocked this bore too, and around 1937 a six- by four-foot shaft was sunk nearby to a depth of some 113 feet, where good water was found.

In 1920 Frank planted more Grenache and some Mataro on five acres of Section 108, an area known as the 'Other Side'. Some three acres of Mataro were also planted behind the cottage and Frank's new house. This was known, not surprisingly, as the 'Back of the House' block. The major planting in 1920 was Shiraz on the sandy slope north of the scrub in Section 118. Known then as the 'Young Shiraz', the block covered 14 acres with 11-foot rows. This activity and the Miltons' original plantings resulted in plantings of 90 acres of vines, consisting of 52 acres of Shiraz, 20 acres of Mataro, 12 acres of Grenache and 6 acres of currants. There was also about a quarter acre of Gordo Muscatels and a few other vines including less than an acre of table grapes. The family looked forward each year to the ripening of the Muscatels, Lady's Fingers, Red Prince, Sultanas, Sweetwaters and Black Turks. Nearby a robust orchard produced almonds, apples, limes, plums, oranges and apricots.

'Soldier vignerons'

In the last years of the Great War, the Australian government began to consider offering assistance to returning servicemen to help re-establish them in civilian life. Pressure built for soldiers to be given the chance to own some land. This well-intentioned scheme was not always successful for a variety of reasons, including the often poor choice of land. Coincidentally irrigated land was available in the Murray Basin at this time. The development of irrigation systems using the waters of the Murray River had had a chequered history since the arrival of the Chaffey brothers in the late 1880s. Periods of booming prices for the produce from Mildura and Renmark contrasted with times of depression, and growers had much to learn about production and marketing. The South Australian and Victorian governments and later the new Commonwealth and the New South Wales governments all participated from the beginning in the Soldier Settler scheme. Their involvement increased with the settlement of ex-servicemen on irrigation blocks, many of which included grape vines.

Many blocks in the McLaren Vale were allocated to and taken up by ex-servicemen. At the McLaren Vale poultry show in August 1921, in a self-congratulatory speech punctuated by frequent applause, a Mr Pocock made several important points about the wine industry and soldier-settlers. In proposing a toast, the speaker opined that after a long residence in the district he had seen the industry grow from a small beginning to 'great proportions'. The industry, he said, was 'in the hands of men who knew how to manage it properly, and make it a success for everyone in South Australia'.[26] The viticultural industry was emerging from a 'period of incubation' and was now on a sound footing. The report in the *Australian Brewing and Wine Journal* captures the mood of the audience:

> *… during the many years to come [it] would require the untiring energy of men where initiative was not paralysed by precedent. [Applause] At the present moment there are roughly about 32,000 acres under vines in South Australia, and about 60,000 in the whole of the Commonwealth … And of those who returned 800 were settled in South Australia growing vines and fruit trees. [Applause] Australia could offer no occupation which showed a better return for well-expended brains and energy than vine-growing. [Applause]*[27]

Mr Pocock trusted that it would be possible to include the viticultural industry on their toast list for hundreds of years to come.

In contrast to the satisfaction felt by many grape growers and winemakers, the Temperance movement, in a nationalistic article published in the same month, questioned the loyalty of the returned soldiers who had gone into the grape-growing or winemaking business. The Temperance movement — mainly the Woman's Christian Temperance Union and the Rechabites — had successfully campaigned for prohibition of the sale of alcoholic beverages on Sunday and after 6.00 pm in the afternoon. These laws led to Australia's notorious 'six o'clock swill', the practice whereby customers would rush to the pub after work and consume alcohol heavily and rapidly in anticipation of the 6.00 pm closing. South Australia was the first state to introduce it as a war austerity measure.[28] This attack on ex-servicemen prompted the editors of the *Australian Brewing and Wine Journal* to applaud the efforts of 'Soldier Vignerons', claiming that some of the most effective responses to the drink problem were coming from returned soldiers who had seen that in countries such as France, where wine is a national drink, there was actually less drunkenness than in countries where the chief beverages are non-alcoholic:

Fortunately for us in Australia, returned soldiers are anything but imbeciles, and with the wider outlook gained by travel and experience, they can take at their real value the arguments put forward by those whose whole horizon is bounded by the view-point of a Band of Hope.[29]

Rejecting the proposition of the Temperance movement and prohibitionists that winemaking was a doomed business in Australia, the writer pointed out that the production of wine in Australia had increased substantially by 1918–19. More importantly, the 'diggers' who were capable of looking after themselves during the Great War could surely be trusted to select an industry to 'gain a peaceful livelihood without requiring advice from such a frankly biased source as a prohibition alliance'.[30] The issue remained current into 1928 when the *Adelaide Notes* concluded that the wine industry held the fortunes of many returned men, and that their interests should be considered.[31]

Despite the complacent tone and moral support for the ex-servicemen, in reality the story was not all good for the industry. While exports of Australian fortified wines to the United Kingdom increased again after the war, large stocks had accumulated and there were prospects of still more as the ex-servicemen's blocks came into production. The wine industry faced problems in the early 1920s, as has been documented by other writers. To help Australian exports compete with the lower transport costs faced by European producers, the Australian government passed the Wine Export Bounty Act in 1924. The bounty was two shillings and nine pence per gallon, with a refund of one shilling and threepence of the excise paid on the fortifying spirit used in making the wine — a total of four shillings per gallon; in 1927 this bounty was reduced by one shilling.

In 1925 the British government introduced a system of preferences for Empire wines: those not exceeding 27 per cent of proof spirit would pay a duty of two shillings per gallon, and for those above, but not exceeding 42 per cent, the duty would be four shillings; non-Empire wines faced a duty

of three shillings per gallon for wines up to 25 per cent and eight shillings up to 42 per cent proof. Preferential access to Australia's largest wine export market and the Australian export bounty had the desired effect. From a low of just over 530 000 gallons in 1922, imports into the United Kingdom increased as follows:

1923	706 510 GALLONS
1924	823 982 GALLONS
1925	1 028 464 GALLONS
1926	1 756 746 GALLONS
1927	4 224 504 GALLONS
1928	1 739 245 GALLONS
1929	2 093 459 GALLONS[32]

From grape growing to winemaking

Australian exports continued through the Depression years, although the volume figures tell us little about the prices received. Given the prosperous 1920s, the Australian bounty and British Imperial preferences, Frank began to think about entering the winemaking business himself. He had been selling his grapes to local winemakers, especially to Thomas Hardy & Sons, Penfolds, Emu, Angoves and Stephen Smith & Co., who owned Tatachilla; to Ryecroft's under its original owner, F W W Wilkinson. He also sold to T C Walker and J C Ingoldby, who bought Ryecroft in 1919. In those days Ryecroft sold virtually all their wine to England, the market for much of McLaren Vale's production.

In 1927 Frank's brother-in-law and wine industry mentor Sam Tolley encouraged him to start producing his own wine. Frank was convinced, and Tolley set about helping him make the shift. In preparation for a change of direction and for his new venture, in 1927 Frank spent some time at Ryecroft learning 'on the job' about winemaking.

Tolley was largely responsible for the design of the winery, which began with storage for 40 000 gallons.[33] The Tolley family had been in the liquor business in South Australia since 1888 when, with Thomas Scott, brothers Ernest (Sam's father) and Douglas Tolley bought a distillery in Adelaide. In 1908 they bought a winery and vineyard in Nuriootpa in the Barossa Valley and they gradually increased their vineyard holdings to 600 acres. Sam Tolley was a director of the firm in the 1920s and chairman for nearly 30 years. He was also chairman of the South Australian Vine Growers Association and president of the then Viticultural Council, so clearly a useful friend to turn to for advice. Construction of the Osborn winery began late in 1927 and in just six weeks it was ready to handle the 1928 vintage. Sam Tolley knew his business and would have been fully aware of Australia's position as an exporter to Britain. He probably saw an opportunity for his friend to expand and also benefit from the changing export market.

In the postwar years, especially from 1924 onwards when the Australian government was 'bent on increasing wine exports in a buoyant post-War market',[34] the British market was sympathetic towards Australian wine, especially fortifieds. Unprecedented amounts of Australian 'port types' were imported into London,

which inevitably caused a surplus years later. History has a habit of repeating itself in these matters. Nevertheless, winemakers in Australia and wine importers in London jumped at the opportunity. Money was to be made from both importing and exporting wine. The combination of Imperial preference and a decrease in the wine bounty hastened the planting of further vineyards. The years 1926 and 1927 saw tremendous growth in the industry. In 1927 total wine production in Australia was 20 million gallons, of which 4 million gallons were exported to Great Britain. In South Australia, production had increased from 12 074 874 gallons in 1926 to 16 179 595 in 1927, making it the premier wine-producing state in Australia.[35]

South Australia was showered with soaking 'bountiful rains' in June 1928 and viticulturalists were kept busy. Despite the good rains and the favourable exporting conditions, Frank's friend and neighbour Herbert Kay, of Amery Vineyards and president of the South Australian Vinegrowers' Association, considered that the year 'had been a most difficult one for the viticultural industry'. What did he mean? His thoughts on the decisions of the government and the introduction of legislation reducing the wine bounty from one shilling and ninepence to one shilling per gallon were recorded in the *Wine and Spirit News and Australian Vigneron*. He believed the government had 'taken the whole trade by surprise'. Coming on the eve of vintage, this 'resulted in a very difficult position' for winemakers. He hoped the government would find a more rational method of fixing grape prices as the winemakers were suffering financially.[36] This was 1928, and the Depression was just around the corner.

Naturally matters viticultural were discussed within the pages of the trade magazine and while it may at first glance appear to be a surprising place to find an article about the Myer Emporium Ltd of Melbourne, perhaps it was not so surprising after all. The September 1928 edition of *Wine and Spirit News and Australian Vigneron* carried the story:

> *That the Myer Emporium Ltd, of Melbourne, has decided to open in Adelaide is, a significant gesture of faith in the city and the State. Myers have taken 200,000 £1 ordinary (the whole issue), in James Marshall & Co. Ltd., the Rundle Street drapers, and propose rebuilding on a large scale. The purchase gives Myers control of Marshall's, and the huge deal, coming at this juncture, should act as a tonic to the ultra-pessimistic.*[37]

It was a significant event for the retail trade in Adelaide. The South Australian wine industry was still relatively small in the 1920s, and everyone knew the major and minor players. The relationship between the Marshalls, the Tolleys and the Osborns would have been well known; possibly for this reason the industry journal chose to highlight this event.

We can imagine that in 1927 Frank was excited about his new winemaking venture. The winery, built in time for the 1928 vintage, was compact, with a row of nine five-ton open fermenting tanks, a block of 19 concrete storage tanks totalling some 40000 gallons and hand-operated basket presses. The roof of the storage block provided working space and some room for wood storage. The fermenting tanks on the lower level, each of 1200 gallons, were filled by a must pump from the pit beneath the Whitehill crusher. Copper water coolers controlled the temperatures, and after the juice had been pumped out the residue was forked

into round wooden cages mounted on wheeled bases that ran along a tramway to the press. A short spur line, complete with 'points', allowed the empty cage to pass the full one (there were only two). Outside vintage time, this system was a source of great amusement for Rowen and d'Arry when they were small children.

For his first vintage in 1928, with assistance from Geoff Kay, Frank produced a heavy dry red and a port, made entirely for the export market to cash in on the Commonwealth export bounty of four shillings per gallon.[38] Geoff Kay lived at Clark Hill (now Coriole Vineyards) and also managed what later became Seaview Winery. For the first 11 vintages, Frank also had the assistance and experience of Harold James ('Lidge') Liddiard. Described as 'a promising cellar hand', Liddiard had come to Osborn from Hardy's, where he had worked for many years. The original fermenting and storage tanks purchased by Frank in 1928 still remain in use at d'Arenberg, although the crusher has been replaced and an improved cooling system installed. The original press, operated by two men (and during the Second World War by the children's nanny, Mickie), was replaced in 1960 by a hydraulic press and the tramway was concreted over.

The construction of the winery in 1927 probably sealed the fate of the six acres of currants inherited from the Milton plantings. It was traditionally believed that currant flavour was too difficult to blend out. Frank pulled down two of the three open-sided currant-drying sheds and used some of the materials in building the winery. During the Second World War, when currants were a controlled product and had to be dried, he arranged for one of his crops to be dried in his neighbour's shed. The block of currants, which for years had been dried by Crowe & Newcombe and its successor, The McLaren Vale Fruit Packers Co-operative, was finally grubbed out in 1957. For its first vintage Bundarra Vineyards produced a Burgundy made from Grenache, Claret made from Shiraz and port types of wine; some of the 1928 and later vintages were exported to P B Burgoyne & Company in London, for decades the UK's biggest importer of Australian wines.[39] Nineteen twenty-eight was not one of the best or most profitable years to be entering the wine industry as a producer. The final report by the Federal Viticultural Council of Australia showed that South Australia's yield for 1927–28 was in fact four and a half million gallons less than the previous vintage. This was caused by severe frosts during September and October, and a lack of seasonal rain.

Despite the seasonal variations and economic outlook, Frank Osborn's work was soon noticed, however, and Bundarra Vineyards was featured in the 1928 publication *Vines and Vineyards of South Australia*, compiled by O L Zeigler and published by the Mail Newspaper Pty Ltd, Adelaide. The two-page spread includes a panoramic photograph of the 'wide expanse of highly productive vineyards', a shot of the house and another of a grape crusher. This feature provides a wonderful snapshot of the vineyard in 1928:

Mr F E Osborn has paid every attention to the land, and there are now 90 acres planted with vines, and a further 70 partly cleared. The vineyard is laid out in sections according to the type of vine, Grenache covering 12 acres, Mataro 20 acres, Shiraz 52 acres and Currants six acres. Both Burgundy and Port types of wine are made, and are utilized entirely for overseas export. The Shiraz vines are planted on high trellises and the currants are grown on the more elevated areas. The vines are usually very healthy, but are sometimes affected with downy mildew and to

counteract the disease a spray of Bordeaux mixture is applied, this proving an
effective means of restraining the attacks. Frosts are rarely known to affect the
vines in this area. The total vintage is stored in cellars on the estate, the capacity
of the tanks being 50,000 gallons. Cement storage is the general type used, and
when extensions, that are now in hand, have been completed the volume will be
considerably increased. The average crop from which the wine is produced is
186 tons, while an additional yield of currants is taken from the vines.[40]

The climate and landscape are described — the land in the vicinity of the vineyard as undulating to hilly, with a sandy inclined soil, and a subsoil consisting chiefly of ironstone, but with portions of limestone. The ironstone, it is emphasised, is good for 'imparting a good body and colour to the grapes'. The rainfall of approximately 22½ inches per year is noted, as is the fact that a further supply of water was accessed by means of a bore. Zeigler concludes that the situation is particularly suited to producing full-bodied wine grapes such as Shiraz, with the average of nine tonnes to the acre and 15½ Baume during a good season. 'Although the estate is barely 17 years old the improvements that have been made, together with the quality of the vintage, speak well for the future that is in store for the young industry so well commenced.[41] It is interesting that the author points out the significance of Bundarra's soil, especially the ironstone, as well as the climate and rainfall. Might he have discussed these issues with Frank when compiling the story, or did he already know about the particular soils of McLaren Vale?

Now determined to build up Bundarra Vineyards, Frank approached the Bank of Adelaide for additional finance. To his surprise and confusion he was refused a loan. Clearly the bank manager had not read Zeigler's glowing review of the vineyard and its owner! At the time he approached the bank, Frank could not have known of the success of his 1928 and earlier vintages. Despite his own success, the prevailing negative outlook worked against him. Nevertheless Frank managed to negotiate overdraft facilities with the English, Scottish and Australian (ES&A) Bank in Adelaide. Although the pressure of his overdraft with the ES&A worried him for the next decade, wine production continued to grow, with bulk sales to larger companies in the district. It was an auspicious beginning for the young winery and its inexperienced proprietor.

CHAPTER 3

Private and public lives

Toni, Rowen and d'Arry Osborn grew up knowing little of their mother, who died when they were so very young. Rowen, who has gathered the family history over the past three decades, had only sparse knowledge of his mother as a young woman. Two photographs of her remain in the family records. One was taken around 1910, when she was about 15 years old. The second was taken when she was 20: it shows a striking looking young woman of medium height and auburn hair, slim in stature, sitting with great composure. She gazes confidently and directly into the camera. In the age of the internet, it has been possible to add to the family's limited knowledge of her life. A search through newspapers dating back to the nineteenth century and early twentieth century has added to the family's limited knowledge of her life.

Born in Adelaide on 26 September 1895, Frances Helena (always known as Helen) d'Arenberg was the oldest child of Frederick Augustus and Eva Roubel (née Williams) d'Arenberg. Helen's arrival in 1895 was noted modestly. The birth announcement in the *Advertiser* simply stated: 'D'Arenberg. On 26 September at Miller Street, North Unley, the wife of F A d'Arenberg, M.A., a daughter.'[1] The d'Arenbergs' second child, George Englebert, was born in 1903. Helen lived at home with her parents at 44 Miller Street until she married Frank Osborn.

Helen d'Arenberg — a life in fragments

Fragments of Helen's early life have been found in diaries and personal letters, and through them we catch glimpses of her as she grew up. When she was 14 months old, Helen's mother visited McLaren Vale, an excursion recorded in the Kay Diaries.[2] In November 1896 Eva d'Arenberg travelled with Helen from Adelaide to Noarlunga, where they were met by Miss Rose Kay and taken to Amery, the Kay brothers' McLaren Vale winery. The diary entry simply states: 'Mrs d'Arenberg and baby arrived by morning coach. E R Kay meeting them at Noarlunga'.[3] Helen, at five, is mentioned in a letter written on 3 July 1900 by her aunt Mary Williams to her fiancé, William Hay. Mary describes how she and her two brothers (aged six and nine) spent the morning shopping in town with Eva and their young cousin Helen.

Helen probably attended Miss Thornber's School located behind Woodspring, where her mother had grown up; records no longer exist as the school closed in 1907. From there, according to family friend Molly Bowen, she went to Halberstate School run by Miss Meeks at 93 Jeffcott Street, North Adelaide. When she was almost 13 years old, Helen, along with 700 to 800 other children, attended a children's fancy dress ball. Hosted by the Lord Mayor of Adelaide, Mr A W Ware CMG, on 26 June 1908, the usual mayoral ball was followed by a fancy dress carnival for the children. The Adelaide *Advertiser* enthused:

> *That the ball was a brilliant success is a mild way of describing it. It was a fairy revel, a picture of fascinating interest and kaleidoscopic colours, a fantasy to captivate*

the youthful imagination, a harmony of sweet sounds and charming spectacular
effects. The parents and guardians of the youthful revellers, many of whom stayed to
watch the scene, were as much entranced as their charges, and equally bewildered by
the magnificent spectacle — the myriad of brilliant fairy lights...[4]

Helen's cousins Jack and Robin Laurie, her future brother-in-law Sam Tolley, future wine man Thomas Hardy (the third), Eric and Syd Hamilton, and some future McLaren Vale friends of the Osborns were also there. In 1912 Helen sat the Junior Public Examination and passed three subjects only: English Literature, Geography and French.[5]

When she was 21 years of age, Helen's name appears once again in the local paper, assisting her mother with patriotic war duties. In May 1916 her mother arranged a bridge afternoon at their home in Miller Street in aid of the Wayville branch of the Red Cross Society. 'Grand slams were pursued in two rooms for a while, and, during an interval, a delicious afternoon tea was served.' The paper noted that the hostess was wearing a frock of black taffeta with a bodice of white ninon while 'Miss Helena d'Arenberg was a dainty figure in a confection of palest pink'.[6] A few weeks later, in early June, Helen, together with her cousins Eileen and Vera Tolley, attended a luncheon party hosted by Mrs S J Asher at the Grand Central Hotel. The following evening she was one of a large audience to attend the opening of the Majestic Theatre in King William Street, Adelaide. Among the guests, family and friends included Mrs Eldin Moulden, Mr and Mrs Albion Tolley, Private Eric Tolley, Mr Jack Tolley and Miss Poppy Tolley.[7] Retired Adelaide journalist Elizabeth Auld remembers Helen as a young woman.

Helen was a friend of Elizabeth's cousin Patrick Auld. In 1993, then aged over 90, Elizabeth recalled that as a young girl she sat on a tram opposite Helen and was 'unable to take her eyes off her because she was so attractive'.[8] Certainly, in the few photographs of Helen as a young woman she presents a very memorable figure.

A keen pianist, Helen studied Pianoforte in 1910 and Piano in 1911 at the Elder Conservatorium of Music, Adelaide University. Her teacher was Bryceson Treharne. The announcement of one occasion in which she took part in a recital at Queen's Hall was published in *The Register* on 14 November 1917. The 'soiree musicale et dansante' was arranged by Mrs H Teesdale Smith assisted by Miss Dorothy Deeley. The recital and dance exhibition was given in aid of the French Red Cross under the patronage and in the presence of His Excellency the Governor and Lady Galway.

Miss Dorothy Deeley will stage three dances, to be performed by 30 of her students. The orchestra will play under the direction of Miss Sylvia Whitington, A.M.U.A.[9] and the accompanists are Miss Lily Sara, A.M.U.A., Miss Helena d'Arenberg, Miss Helen Hall, and Mr Frank Holman.[10]

Although she had not attained the letters A.M.U.A after her name, when she travelled to London Helen studied briefly at the Trinity College of Music, London. A record of her time there was among many lost during the Second World War. Trinity College of Music was established in 1842 to ensure a high standard of skilled teaching and music examination in London. Examiners were soon 'eagerly sought and gratefully welcomed' not only in all parts of Great Britain but also in the Dominions.[11]

RIGHT *Joe Osborn in his Norwood Football Club strip.*

ABOVE *Frank Osborn (middle row, far right), one of the 'Ruffians' of 1909, second-year medical students, Adelaide University.*

LEFT *Frank Osborn (far left, back row), and the 1910 Inter-Varsity Cricket Team.*

ABOVE *Helen d'Arenberg, aged 20, c. 1915.*

BELOW *The Osborn children on the beach in 1929.*
L to R: Rowen (aged 4), d'Arry (2), Toni (7).

LEFT *Osborn children in 1934. L to R: d'Arry (aged 7), Toni (12), Rowen (9).*

ABOVE *Frank Osborn, aged 42, in 1930.*

ABOVE *Lieutenant Toni Osborn, WANS, 1940s.*

ABOVE *Edith Athelstan Clark (Mickie), 1942.*

Aerial view of Bundarra Vineyards and homestead, 1939.

ABOVE *Making a haystack,*
Bundarra, 1944. L to R:
d'Arry, Norm King, Rowen.

RIGHT *The Osborns at 'Kurrajong',*
Payneham, South Australia, 1948.
L to R: Corporal Ian Marshall,
Aunt Edith Tolley, Flight Lieutenant
John Felstead, Grannie (Mary)
Osborn, Aunt Mary Marshall
(standing at rear).

RIGHT *Lunch at the High Commissioner's Residence, Karachi, 26 December 1950. Rowen Osborn, Third Secretary, Australian High Commission, is seated at the head of the table, and Prime Minister RG Menzies is third on Rowen's left.*

RIGHT *Frank Osborn with Beverley and Rowen Osborn on their Wedding Day, 25 January 1956.*

ABOVE *d'Arry and Pauline's wedding day, 16 August 1958, at St Columba's Church, Hawthorn, Adelaide, 1976.*

ABOVE *Chester Osborn at 12 months, 1963.*

BELOW *Jackie (17) and Chester (14) at home, 1976.*

RIGHT *d'Arry Osborn (centre) entertains entrants in the 1969 Miss World Competition during a Bacchus Club function held in Jim Ingoldby's garden in McLaren Flat.*

RIGHT *d'Arry in the vineyard pouring a glass of 1970 Burgundy, 1973.*

ABOVE *d'Arry showing off the Michael Frangos Trophy for best vintage port at The Royal Queensland Wine Show, 1978.*

When she left Adelaide for Liverpool via Durban on Wednesday, 14 May 1919,[12] Helen was already engaged to Frank Osborn. It is not known how they met and we know nothing of their engagement; it seems it remained a secret for some time. A formal newspaper announcement has not been found. The family speculate that Helen's grandmother Eva Roubel Williams was not happy about the event. In a letter to his son Rowen dated 9 February 1957, Frank recalled the first occasion he had taken Helen to the winery 38 years before:

This day 38 years ago was also a Saturday and a most important one in the lives of Helen and myself when she gave a morning tea party at The Bohemian and wore her ring in public for the first time. Only Bay [Baylis English] knew anything about our engagement. In the afternoon we came out here and walked all over the property and I remember Helen crying while we were in the currants partly, she told me, because she was so happy and partly at the step she had taken ...[13]

Perhaps her overseas trip was to be used as an opportunity to consider her future. If the engagement was kept secret for some time, it is possible that Helen herself had doubts. Frank may not have been her only suitor. Family folklore has it that Dr John Mayo, younger brother of women's medical practitioner Dr Helen Mayo, was at one stage deeply in love with Helen. It seems his family were reluctant that John should marry, and in fact he remained unmarried. He and Helen probably met because he lived near the home of the d'Arenbergs' family friend Tom Bowen. As she set out overseas, Helen was farewelled at the ship by her friends, who teased her that she would forget Frank and meet someone else on her grand tour.

Helen was, after all, an intelligent, accomplished and attractive woman. The story has it that she turned to her friend Girlie Wertheim and said, 'You believe I'll come back and marry him, don't you?' Girlie replied that of course she would and that the Wertheims (who produced and sold pianos in Adelaide) would present her with a piano as a wedding gift. Helen did receive a Bechstein three-quarter grand piano as a wedding gift: it remains at McLaren Vale.

While in Europe Helen visited Paris, where she met with hostility when signing a hotel register: it seems some of the d'Arenbergs had sided with Germany during the war. In England Helen became friendly with her cousin Ella Frances Kelly, who in 1919 married her cousin, Ignatius George Kelly, the eldest son of Professor David Kelly and Sophie Armstrong d'Arenberg Kelly. After almost a year overseas Helen returned to Australia on the *Orsova*; she arrived on Monday, 10 May 1920, and married Frank Osborn six weeks later.

Marriage, home and children

Frank and Helen were married at St Peter's College Chapel on 24 June 1920, the service conducted by Reverend K J F Bickersteth, then in his first year as headmaster of the school. Bickersteth wrote the words 'old scholar' above the entry in the marriage register. Frank, of course, was not an old scholar, but the use of the chapel was granted in recognition that Helen's grandfather had been headmaster of the school. Her mother had also married in the chapel in 1894. Frank and Helen's wedding was small. The best man was Sam Tolley, who had

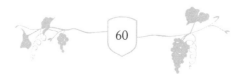

been a fellow officer in the 43rd Battalion; Sam became Frank's brother-in-law when he married his sister Edith only a few months later, on 20 November 1920. Helen's close friend Baylis English, known later to Frank's children as Auntie Bay, was her bridesmaid. The couple honeymooned at Melbourne's Menzies Hotel.

Helen and Frank Osborn set about furnishing their new home at McLaren Vale and establishing a garden. Their wedding gifts, including a dining-room suite from the Marshalls, a silver-framed tantalus with two cut-glass decanters from the Tolleys, a dinner service from Frank's school friend Dr Charlie Drew and his wife and various EPNS dishes, helped greatly. They were evidently anticipating children, as from the outset the walls of the second bedroom were decorated with a children's frieze.

The garden included lawn and flowerbeds, and soon a fishpond with a bridge was added. Cypress hedges enclosed an orchard with plum, orange and apricot trees. In the back garden, trees provided shelter from the north wind and enclosed a back garden and clotheslines. Later a large trellis was built over the motor shed's driveway.[14] Climbing roses covered it; in later years it shaded the car when not garaged. An arch along the footpath leading to the garage from the house was eventually covered by creepers, while another section of the path had post-and-wire trellises on each side planted with climbing roses, of which Frank's favourite was 'Black Boy'. Roses were planted in most parts of the garden. Two golden cypresses marked each side of the driveway that circled the front lawn. The southern edge of the garden was marked by a row of yellow broom. An aviary was built on the western side of the house, its west wall and roof constructed of small pieces of corrugated tin. Later the wire covered part of the enlarged aviary.

A shade house for ferns and pot plants was added to the northern end of the side verandah and a small bed of Cecil Brunner roses was also planted. Later known as 'Mummie's roses', these were probably chosen by Helen.

Fruit trees were planted in other parts of the garden as well as in the orchard. Two prunus grew in the lee of the northern hedge and two plum trees in the backyard. Passionfruit flourished on a wire trellis around the semi-underground tank. Dirt paths linked and set off the different parts of the garden (later some of these were bricked and others covered with white barytes metal). Maintaining the garden occupied much of the couple's spare time, although gardeners would have done some of the work.

Frank's father, Joseph, died on 25 May 1921, aged 69 years. Given his past propensity for self-promotion, it is somewhat surprising to find that an obituary did not appear in the wine press. Nevertheless, a funeral card 'In Loving Remembrance' honours the man who was the 'Dearly loved husband of Mary Jane Osborn'. The prayer indicates the love and respect with which he was held:

> *Peaceful be thy silent slumber,*
> *Peaceful in thy grave so low;*
> *Thou no more wilt join our number,*
> *Thou no more our song wilt know.*
> *Yet again we hope to meet thee,*
> *When the day of life is fled,*
> *And in heaven with joy to greet thee,*
> *Where no farewell tears are shed.*

Joseph did not live to see the arrival of his first grandchild, Jane Antoinette (Toni), born on 9 September 1921 at around 5 am at the Memorial Hospital, Adelaide. Jane was one of her Osborn grandmother's names and Antoinette occurs in the d'Arenberg family, but not among the Abeltshausers (see p. 116). Helen liked the shortening of Antoinette to Toni. Surprisingly, no photographs of Toni as a baby survive. The Osborn children's collective memories retain only one anecdote of her babyhood. Toni was in a pram on the lawn between the house and the aviary when a snake appeared on the grass near her pram. The family owned a dog at the time that chased away or killed the snake, thus achieving hero status in Rowen Osborn's eyes from the time he heard the story as a small boy.

Rowen Frederick Osborn was born on 10 November 1924 at the Wakefield Street Private Hospital. At 10¼ pounds, he was the heaviest Osborn baby. He was named Rowen for his racehorse-owning grandfather and his great-great-grandfather Rowe; Frederick was his grandfather d'Arenberg's first name. Rowen was born around 7.30 in the morning, a time he now considers 'unadventurous', quite unlike his own life as a diplomat. Photographs of Toni and Rowen as small children, taken in the garden at 'Darroch', the Marshalls' home at Payneham, survive in the family album. In one, Rowen was a curly-haired one year old. One of his earliest memories, outside Grannie Osborn's house, is of his Aunty Edith (Mrs Sam Tolley) asking what had become of his curls after they had been cut off. While it was Helen's intention to shorten Antoinette to Toni, the toddlers found this difficult to pronounce. Toni became 'Tooks' or, as Rowen preferred, 'Toodie'. In return, Toni gave her brother the nickname 'Tow', but he insisted on being called Rowen when he began school.

Tragedy

On 27 December 1926 Frank and Helen's third child, Francis d'Arenberg Osborn, was born at Wakefield Street Private Hospital. He has always been known as d'Arry, in the same way Helen's mother Eva d'Arenberg was always known as Mrs d'Arry. Helen had been admitted to hospital a few days earlier before the birth but had been discharged over Christmas and went to stay in Adelaide with Frank's mother. Mary Osborn, by then widowed, was living at Payneham. The two eldest children were also staying there. Toni, who was five years old, recalls her grandmother and great-aunt making peach jam at the time. When they asked Toni to stay and talk to her mother, she is said to have replied that she was 'too busy' and then run off to play again outside. Within hours of d'Arry's birth, Frank, who had been at his wife's bedside at the hospital, became concerned by her loss of colour and growing distress. He called hospital staff, who found she was haemorrhaging. Dr Verco, her GP, was called in from a golf game and a blood transfusion was arranged using Frank's blood. Medical understanding of blood groups was not then as developed as it is now and the transfusion failed through incompatibility. Helen died on the day her son was born.

Helen's funeral, which left from 'Darroch' on the afternoon of Wednesday, 28 December, was held at the North Road Cemetery at Nailsworth. The notice in the Adelaide *Advertiser* referred to it as a 'motor' funeral, indicating to those attending that they would travel by car. Frank later told the children that the hearse broke down on the way to 'Darroch' and so arrived late, which he felt sure would have amused his wife. After Helen's death Toni and Rowen returned to McLaren Vale with their father. Baby d'Arry and the nurse Frank engaged stayed for a few months with the Marshall household at Payneham, where two rooms were set aside for them, one painted as a nursery for the duration of their stay. 'Darroch', purchased by James and Mary Marshall in 1919, was a large mansion of 22 rooms; it easily accommodated the four Marshall children, d'Arry and his nurse.

Following Helen's death Frank's family were anxious that he should find someone suitable to care for the children. His mother, her unmarried sister Robina and a friend of Helen's, Bay English, decided to rotate visits to McLaren Vale to help look after Toni and Rowen. When Mary Marshall, Frank's sister, heard about an English nanny, Edith Athelstan Clark, who had been looking after the children of a family near Gawler, north of Adelaide, she contacted and interviewed her. Mary was very impressed, and after a few enquiries she encouraged Frank to engage her as nanny, which he did.

After a short stay at 'Darroch', getting to know d'Arry, in June 1927, she and the three children (Toni and Rowen had come for a visit) travelled home to McLaren Vale. Toni and Rowen remember their first meeting with Miss Clark, who thereafter was known by all the family as 'Mickie', and the automobile journey home. Mickie reached over to the back seat, extending her free hand to the two small children; she held their tiny hands in hers, forming a lifelong bond between them. Mickie became part of the family, remaining with them until 1958 when d'Arry married at the age of 32.

Mickie

Born on 18 October 1888 at Bootle near Liverpool in Lancashire, Edith was the eldest of four children born to Edward Athelstan Clark and Edith May (née Barber). Her father, who graduated from Cambridge University, was the curate of Christ's Church, Bootle. Her sister, Gladys, was born in 1891 and her brothers, Thomas Edward and John, were born in 1892 and 1898 respectively. She was educated at home by her parents and tutors, partly because her father's position as a clergyman meant the family relocated frequently. From Bootle they moved to Henbury in Gloucestershire (1889–91), Bristol (1892–97), Didbrook in Gloucestershire (1898), Ingham in Suffolk (1899–1902) and Leavesden Asylum, Kings Langley, Hertfordshire (1903–12), where the Reverend Clark was chaplain. Around 1912 Edward Clark left the Church and his marriage and moved north to live in Wallasey, a resort town in Cheshire. This became Mickie's home too, although she had enrolled at the Norland Institute for Training Children's Nurses in Pembroke Square, Bayswater, in London. While she studied in London, Mickie recalled, her father would visit and they would go out to little Italian restaurants in Soho, which she found fascinating. She later retained her interest in the Norland Institute and regularly received a quarterly journal containing news of women who had trained there.

Mickie left the Institute for her first appointment as a nanny to the Pearman family, who lived in Edward Square, Kensington. Mr Pearman worked for the Foreign Office. The household staff included a butler, cook, scullery maid and housemaid, and a nursery maid to assist her as nanny. Mrs Pearman also had her own *femme de chambre* or personal maid. Mickie's charge was one delicate baby whom she often pushed in its pram up the Cromwell Road to Kensington Gardens.

By the time war was declared on 3 August 1914 Mickie had returned to her father at Wallasey. Among her correspondents at the time were two soldiers, to one of whom, Pat Paterson, she became engaged. In due course his regiment, the Liverpool Scottish, was sent to France. This may have been the reason she also went to France in late 1914 to take up a position in the household of William Kissam Vanderbilt. In the fashion of some American families, there were two William Kissam Vanderbilts, father and son, designated I and II. The father was 65 years of age in 1914, the son 36. In a copy of Edwin J Hoyt's 1963 publication *The Vanderbilts and Their Fortunes*, Mickie underlined references to both father and son and their families. The father, whose grandfather had founded the Vanderbilt fortune, inherited $65 million and made vast gifts to his children. According to Hoyt, he spent much of his time at his chateau, which he had bought in the 1890s, in Normandy. By April 1915 Mickie was a nanny for Madame Valton, looking after her baby son and older sister in Avenue Victor Hugo in Paris, but the city was not a safe or comfortable place to be living during the Great War. Madame Valton decided to move her household to Arcachon, a resort town 450 miles south-west of Paris on an inlet from the Bay of Biscay, just 50 miles from Bordeaux. Mickie's fiancé Pat was killed in action in France in July 1916 on the first day of the Allied attack on the Somme.

Her father, Edward, found work with the Royal Army Medical Corps as a ship's doctor, visiting Asian ports as well as Australia. He sent Mickie a postcard from Sydney. When he returned to England he convinced his family — Mickie, his second wife, Ethel, and their son, Edward Herbert, that their future was in

South Australia. They sailed from Glasgow on 29 May 1920 on the *Aeneas*. Once they arrived in Adelaide the family established themselves on a farm at Carey Gully in the Adelaide Hills near Aldgate, raising goats, which was not a success. In the early 1920s they moved to Enfield, where Edward found a position at the Northfield Mental Hospital. He died on 22 October 1937.

Meanwhile Mickie first worked at the Magill Homes in Adelaide, which she did not enjoy, and then began looking for work as a nanny once again. She obtained a position with the Earn Barritt family on a sheep property, Yattalunga, 30 miles north of Adelaide, looking after the young son and daughter of the family. She liked the children but got on less well with their mother, Mrs Jean Barritt, and returned to Adelaide. She may have worked for a time as a waitress at the Piccadilly Tea Rooms on North Terrace. This establishment was operated by a Mrs Twiss and Mrs Eva d'Arenberg, Frank Osborn's mother-in-law, who had been widowed in 1923. The tearooms were reputed to have included some 'society girls' among their staff. It was at the Piccadilly that Mickie remembered once seeing Helen Osborn — little knowing that she would spend the rest of her life so closely involved with Helen's children.

After Frank's death in 1957, and d'Arry's marriage in 1958, Mickie visited England before moving into the McLaren Vale township. She retained close links with the Osborn family until she died in McLaren Vale on 31 July 1978. Following her wishes, her funeral took place at the Crematorium, Centennial Park Cemetery, Adelaide, and her ashes were placed in a rose garden there.

Mickie's influence on the lives of the three Osborn children cannot be underestimated. She was a mother to them, she successfully ran the Osborn home,

and she cared for Frank as he became more ill and frail. She is remembered with great affection by all the family.

Toni, Rowen and d'Arry can only guess at the pain their father suffered over Helen's death. Sadly they have retained no personal recollections of her: she was only 31 years old when she died. It feels to them that they were quickly discouraged from talking about her. This was an accepted method of dealing with the loss of a parent of young children. Mickie lived in the house almost as a surrogate mother, and in time their memories of their mother faded. Frank apparently made no attempt to remarry. It might have been expected that, because of the intimate relationship they shared in raising his three children, he would propose marriage to Mickie. Although she was a highly educated and articulate woman who fitted perfectly into Frank's world, it seems it was not meant to be. She was undoubtedly the mother figure in their lives and it is evident that Mickie had an enormous and positive influence on the children's lives.

Frank displayed photographs of Helen in his bedroom and in the sitting room, where one sat proudly on her piano. There were also two oval miniatures, one of which he always took with him when he was away from home. The children remember a particularly poignant story from the mid 1930s. On a trip to Adelaide to attend a meeting of the State Board of the Returned Sailors', Soldiers' and Airmen's Imperial League of Australia (now the Returned and Services League), of which he was vice-president, his suitcase was stolen from his car. A press report of the incident mentioned that he was especially anxious to recover the miniature of his late wife. The thief was eventually caught but claimed to have thrown the miniature away; it was never recovered.

Public life and the social pages

Soon after his return from the war in 1917, Frank Osborn became involved in the Returned and Services League of Australia (RSL); he became a long-term member and foundation president of the McLaren Vale and District sub-branch of the RSL. Joining in 1919, he was vice-president of the South Australian branch from 1934 to 1940 and served on the committee for 20 years. He played an instrumental role in the construction of the war memorial in front of the McLaren Vale Institute Hall in 1934. The RSL was not the only service club he joined. Frank quickly became a member of the South Australian Legacy Club, the McLaren Vale and District Progress Association, the McLaren Vale School Committee and the Morphett Vale Higher Primary School Committee. He also served on the District Council of Noarlunga. When the Legacy Club held its annual ball on 2 November 1937, Frank was chairman of the ball committee. Perhaps evoking memories of their time in Egypt, the ball featured 'a male ballet in the Dance of Egypt'. This was to be an informal event: 'The Base Commandant (Brigadier A M Martyn) has given permission for mess dress to be worn'. Frank continued his voluntary work in the community; he especially liked organising fundraising events but also contributed with donations. The McLaren Vale Southern Districts War Memorial Hospital Appeal held in December 1947 raised funds from local residents. A donation by the Kay family of £500 was the largest donation, followed by J Ingoldby at £250 and F E Osborn at £50.[15]

Meanwhile the Osborn children had grown up and were making their own way in the world. Toni's career and travels attracted notice in the social pages of the

Adelaide, Canberra and Melbourne newspapers. So too did Rowen's diplomatic career. By contrast, d'Arry's activities at the vineyard began to be reported in the wine press only in the 1950s.

Snippets from Toni Osborn's social life were frequently published in the Adelaide *Advertiser*'s weekly column 'About People by Lady Kitty'. In keeping with the custom and formality of the day, 'Lady Kitty' (whose real name has not been divulged) always referred to Toni as Miss Antoinette Osborn. For example, in October 1945, when Toni hosted a luncheon party at the Gresham Hotel for her friend Helen Chamberlain, who was leaving for Newcastle, Lady Kitty recorded a guest list that included: 'Mesdames Bruce Frayne, Alec Plummer, Dudley Broadbent and Keith Frayne'.[16] This form of address is anachronistic today; in those days, however, women were conventionally identified by their husband's Christian name and surname. The following month, Lady Kitty reported that:

> *To celebrate the 21st birthday of her brother Rowen, Miss Antoinette Osborn will be hostess at a buffet sherry party at the home of their father Mr F E Osborn, McLaren Vale, on Saturday. The 40 young people are invited for 7.00 pm and later in the evening will dance on the verandah. Antoinette will wear an afternoon frock of sky blue with pin tucked bodice.[17]*

Rowen remembers the occasion well, especially the speeches. The article beautifully evokes the era, including ladies' fashion and, importantly, the fashion in party drinks. A description of the hostess's gown when reporting such occasions remained a feature of social pages until at least the 1960s. Given that in the 1950s men

conventionally drank either beer or scotch while women sipped sweet sherry, could it be that the Osborns were ahead of their time by hosting a 'sherry party' in 1945?[18]

In June of the following year, when the British aircraft carrier *Glory* anchored in Outer Harbour, Toni and friends were visiting the ship while newspaper cameramen were busy. A large crowd of 20000 inspected the ship that day, with the Royal Navy providing guides. It was here that Toni and her friends Barbara and Judith Hoar were pictured with a handsome sub-lieutenant who was pointing out an item of interest to them.[19] Social and sporting occasions, as well as several farewell parties leading up to Toni's departure for England, made topical reading for those interested in Adelaide's social life.[20] The Shell Oil Company held a cabaret dinner in September 1946 that was attended by Toni Osborn's party, who were 'in high spirits'. Again Rowen was one of the guests at Toni's table that evening.[21]

On 28 February 1948 Toni left South Australia on board the *Stratheden* for London, where she visited her Australian second cousin Ella Frances Kelly, who would have been a few years older than her mother, Helen, had she lived. Ella had married her cousin, Ignatius George Kelly, the son of Professor Kelly and Sophie d'Arenberg, in April 1919 and they had two children, Kathleen Helen (born 1923) and Dermott Frederick (born 1926). Her husband had died in 1931 and Ella lived for a time in Oxford, where she supported herself by taking in students as paying guests. She then moved to Kensington Gardens, London, where Toni stayed with her. Ella's daughter Kathleen (Katie) worked in the Foreign Office, serving in Ankara under her mother's cousin, Sir David Kelly, who was then ambassador. Toni used Katie's room in her absence and later they shared it while they were both in London.

Toni's overseas travels would have been of great interest to many of the readers of the social pages of the *Advertiser*, and a travelogue can be created from these snippets. Toni remained overseas for almost two years. So interested was the paper in Toni Osborn's experience working in London that the *Advertiser* featured a story on her travels:

> *It is not hard for an Australian girl to work her way through the UK says newly returned Miss Antoinette Osborn of McLaren Vale — provided the girl can type and write shorthand. 'By English standards, the average Australian typist is pretty efficient' said Miss Osborn. 'If she can do shorthand too — which a lot of English typists can't — she finds it very easy to get a job.'*[22]

Before travelling overseas Toni had been a shorthand typist in Adelaide, so she found it very easy to find work in London. And the wages in London, she told the paper, were much better than those in Australia — a great encouragement for others to travel to the UK. Once in England Toni found a position as a private secretary to an executive of Shell Oil. The job took her to a conference in Singapore and after the conference she stayed on at the firm's Singapore branch, where she worked for nearly a year. From Singapore she sailed for Fremantle and transhipped to the *Otranto*, reaching Adelaide in early June 1950. Once she had been home for a few weeks she visited Rowen in Canberra. Watching the Test cricket, acting as hostess to friends at McLaren Vale, speaking at charity lunches, and further trips to Melbourne and Canberra, were all reported as items of interest to readers over the next few years. Toni spent little time in Australia from 1950 onwards.

Following family tradition, Rowen Osborn went to Prince Alfred College before attending the University of Adelaide — he was the first Osborn to complete a degree. Highlights of Rowen's social life and diplomatic career were also featured within the pages of the Adelaide *Advertiser* and the *Canberra Times*.[23] After completing his arts degree, Rowen became a diplomatic student at Canberra University College, graduating in March 1950. His rise through the ranks was rapid. At the time Toni planned to visit him in Canberra, the *Mail* reported, Rowen was hastily packing his bags to join the Australian diplomatic staff in Karachi.[24] Appointed Third Secretary in the Australian High Commission, there he remained until December 1952. Not long before he was due to return to Australia, the *Advertiser* once again had news of both Rowen and Toni, who by then was working in Bangkok:

> *For a long weekend break from her post in Bangkok, Miss Antoinette Osborn flew down to Rangoon to visit her cousin, Miss Kate Kelly. In recent letters to her family, Antoinette says she is applying herself to learning the Siamese language, and still finds life in Siam fascinating. Rowen, who is at the High Commission's office in Karachi, expects to return to SA at the end of January to visit his family at Bundarra, McLaren Vale.*[25]

Rowen did return to McLaren Vale before taking up his next appointment in Canberra, which was as Third Secretary in the Economic and Technical Assistance Branch during 1953 and 1954. The following year he became the Personal Assistant to the Permanent Head of the Department of External Affairs, (later Sir) Arthur Tange, and in 1955 was promoted to External Affairs Officer 2. Further promotion saw Rowen appointed as Second Secretary in the Australian Embassy in The Hague from February 1956 to July 1958. It was while he was at The Hague that Rowen received the moving letter from his father in 1957 recalling the time he had first taken his future wife to the winery. It was also during this time that the *Australian Brewing and Wine Journal* reported on the activities of both the Osborn and Tolley families, and in particular a happy reunion. Rowen had the opportunity to meet with his Aunty Edith because her husband, Sam Tolley, had business in Amsterdam. They met at The Hague before Rowen left for New York to work at the UN General Assembly.

In 1955 Rowen met Beverley Jean Gemmell of Deniliquin in Canberra through a mutual friend. They shared a lift back to Adelaide and love blossomed. They celebrated their engagement on 1 November 1955 and were married at Christ Church, South Yarra, Victoria, on 25 January 1956, before Rowen was posted to Dutch New Guinea. Marriage was in the air, and one year after the death of their father, d'Arry and Toni also married. d'Arry married Pauline Rowland Preston on 16 August 1958. Pauline's family name was known in Adelaide; she was the daughter of Alan Preston, of the firm Coulton, Palmer & Preston of Weymouth Street. Pauline and d'Arry had been friends for many years. Before their marriage Pauline, who trained as a physiotherapist, had travelled around the world and had a distinguished career in London, treating such famous people as Dame Margot Fonteyn, the Duke of Norfolk and other members of the royal family.[26] Soon after d'Arry's marriage on 26 April 1958, Toni Osborn married Patrick Bourne, whom she had met in Singapore.

CHAPTER 4

Bundarra Vineyards, 1943 to 1957

I‍N ACREAGE AND VOLUME, THE AUSTRALIAN WINE INDUSTRY BOOMED IN THE years after the Great War. At the same time, the wine glut depressed prices, even before the onset of the Depression in the 1930s.[1] The boom in volume is attributed to three main factors: the subsidised settlement of returned servicemen, the huge export subsidy for fortified wines and the halving of tariffs in Britain for wines imported from the British Empire.[2] At Bundarra Vineyards, Frank was producing fortified or sweet red and lighter white wines. While very few records from the winery for the interwar period up to 1950 have survived, we know he continued to grow Shiraz, Mataro, Grenache and currants. These grapes were sold to large producers such as Emu Wines, Hamilton Ewell Vineyards, Penfolds, Hardy's and Tatachilla.[3] Some shipments were also made to P B Burgoyne, London.

A modest grape-growing and winemaking business

Frank never fully regained his health after the Great War. He was so ill during 1942 that he crushed no grapes at all so did not have a vintage that year.[4] Wine

77

production ceased and all grapes were sold to other wineries. Full production resumed the following year when d'Arry, who left school at the age of 16, began working in the winery full time to help his father. This was the work he had always wanted to do, so he was happy to leave school behind. As boys he and Rowen had often worked in the winery at weekends. Bundarra still had horses up until the late 1950s; they used them for pulling the burner — the incinerator on wheels they used to burn all the cuttings — until about 1961 when they bought the first rotavator on a diesel tractor. Instead of burning the cuttings, the rotavator chopped them up, which was much faster. The downside of this practice was that after about seven or eight years without burning the cuttings they had diseases in the vineyard they had never seen before, such as downy mildew and powdery mildew.

d'Arry, who has many memories of working at the vineyard both before and after leaving school, recalls:

> We were quite strong and we used to love helping to burn up the cuttings with the incinerator we had in those days, with the workmen here, on the weekends and Easter holidays. We would also help with the vintage… Not that they were very big vintages… 1943 of course was the first year that I was home and we went straight into vintage.[5]

Local Aboriginal people worked on the property, picking grapes at vintage. From the first days Frank owned the vineyard they came up from the Aboriginal Mission at Point McLeay on Lake Alexandrina for work. Some worked very hard, he recounts, but they also liked to play tricks on his father and other vineyard owners in the district. For example, if they were contracted to work at Bundarra

Vineyards, Frank and d'Arry would drive down in their 1926 Bean truck to collect them. 'One of the things which was typical of them…when you brought them over on the truck half of those would clear off and go work somewhere else after they'd come over on a free trip, and the people from the other companies who were doing the same thing, their people came to us. They…treated it like a holiday and like fun. They were very funny, some of them.'[6]

Ploughing the vineyard was another job for young d'Arry. This was tough work because the winery didn't have a tractor; instead they used six Clydesdale horses for the work:

> About 1947, I think it was, Dad bought the first rubber-tyred tractor into this area after the war. Before that there were steel wheels, and we've still [laughs] got the old tractor over in the shed somewhere, and of course that was my pride and joy and great fun to run. I kept the tractor so well that it still works, I think, if you start it up. But that's a Farmall H tractor.[7]

The current tractor museum is a monument to the more than 50 years that d'Arry has collected tractors. He has a story to tell about every tractor in the collection. The purchase of tractors was evidence the family had sufficient money to improve farming and vineyard methods. Winemaking had to be made more cost effective and tractors helped in this. Young d'Arry had other jobs on the farm too:

> It was my job to feed and milk the cows in the morning, and separate the milk, get the cream, and once or twice a week make the butter. We used to sell butter by the

pound to the local delicatessens — with our name on it, dairy butter. The milk was affected by the time of the year. In the wintertime when the cows had the free run of the vineyard there were dandelions, as we called them — actually capeweed I think is its real name — and they used to flavour the milk so it had a nasty taste and the butter would taste funny, so you couldn't use it sometimes for that. Also we had some wild garlic growing down in the vineyard at that stage — there was one patch that had been an old orchard when the property was bought by my father — and if the cows ate that then you had garlic butter and garlic milk. It tasted horrible! The garlic butter wasn't quite so bad when I think back but we didn't use it much. They were the sorts of things that you grow up with and don't forget.[8]

The farm ran cows up until Frank's death. d'Arry remembers that 'in the war years, 1943/44/45, we never got the work done, we never got the pruning done in time no matter how we tried'.[9] Norm King, who worked as foreman for Frank from 1912, also kept cows and sometimes looked after the Osborn stock over the weekend. d'Arry believes Norm had a great influence on their lives. Born in 1888 in the cottage at Hardy's, Norm had worked at Hardy's winery in McLaren Vale. He recalled that when he was eight years old he used to come up to the Milton property with the original Tom Hardy to open the gates for him and drive through the property.

Norm taught Frank and d'Arry everything about planting and caring for the vines and making wine by hand with an old wine press.[10] In d'Arry's words:

Of course Dad didn't know anything about vines, did he, so Norm King had to show him how to do all the vines. I'm sure he was the foreman, and he was still

here when I came home. I didn't know anything about it either, and I didn't know anything about winemaking. Dad didn't tell me anything about winemaking. Norm King showed me how to make the wine. We just followed — we grew up with it — a practice that was over there with an old hand press. That went on until 1960, when we bought a press that was run by a machine — the hydraulic press we still have, the Coq press, which is over 100 years old. Then we bought a Bromley Tregoning press, which was a few years later, and then we built our own presses, which we're very proud of because they're state of the art: copying the old principle but done with hydraulics and electric motors and computers and things. Anyway Norm taught me how to prune vines, and how to work the horses.[11]

At that stage the land consisted of 96 acres of vines and plenty of scrub.

Like his father, d'Arry learned not to spend money unnecessarily, a principle he continues to follow. But he has invested in good equipment when needed. One new technology embraced by d'Arry was the electrification of the production area. In 1951, when grid electricity was connected to the winery, electric generators replaced the old kerosene-run Delco generator:

The Delco was quite good. It ran on power kerosene. You used to start it with petrol. I used to run that, of course, and when I got older I'd pull the head off it and clean up the carb, service all the engines and pull them all to bits.[12]

When d'Arry took over responsibility for the day-to-day operations and full management of the business, Bundarra Vineyards were still producing bulk wine

for sale to the larger producers in South Australia. They exported some to Britain through the Emu Wine Company and P B Burgoyne & Company but also had a small cellar door trade in flagons, for which the winery held a two-gallon licence.

Before the outbreak of the Second World War export sales for Australian wine broke all records, with Britain the main customer. Sweet red wine was then the preferred beverage. In 1939–40 Australia exported more than 3 600 000 gallons of wine. However, in January 1941 the British government placed an embargo on all imports of wine and spirit unless licensed by the Ministry of Food, and Australian exports fell to only 1 550 000 gallons.[13] At Bundarra, wine production continued mainly for bulk sales to larger companies in the district as well as to Hamilton Ewell Vineyards, Glenelg.

By 1946–47 Australian wine exports to Britain increased to a healthy 2 720 598 gallons, but it would be another 40 years before this figure was surpassed. In the late 1940s the Australian export wine industry was drastically reduced as a result of the predictable postwar wine stock build-up in London. This glut was due mainly to lack of bottles but also to a change in British taste and fashion away from heavy Australian sweet wines.

Australia enjoyed decades of postwar economic prosperity. Largely triggered by the sale of wool to Korea during the Korean War, this prosperity helped pay for the massive postwar migration programs that began to change the face of the country and have a profound influence on our attitudes to food and wine.[14] Despite the buoyant economy, however, wine production and plantings remained static during the 1950s. In other words, growth in the wine industry — both domestic and international — was slow. Two main factors explain this situation:

Britain kept tariffs high until the end of the 1950s, and Australia's licensing laws continued to discourage public wine consumption, relative to beer. Indeed, annual wine consumption took until the early 1960s to reach six litres per capita.[15]

d'Arry's diaries

Frank spent much of September, October and November of 1950 in hospital, so it fell to d'Arry to manage work at the winery. It was in 1950 that d'Arry began to keep diaries of his activities, modelled on the Kay Diaries. They were 'rough diaries, the sort of thing that as a young fellow you did. You wrote in how many eggs you got and you milked the cows'.[16] Today d'Arry wishes he had written 'things that mattered', but, although he does not recognise it, the information contained in his diary reveals a great deal about Bundarra, his winemaking and the industry in general. Indeed, the diaries and letters are a bounty for the historian. Transcribed by Rowen, they contain records of the activities of the year including vintage, developmental work, grape varieties, wine sold, farming, employees and wages.

Through d'Arry's diaries a snapshot in time emerges. In 1950 we read that vintage commenced on 27 February when they started picking currants; on 13 March they picked wine grapes and finished picking on 17 April — very similar to today's time frame. Although d'Arry didn't record the weather conditions in his daily diary, Herbert Kay of Kay Brothers did so, and this document is a valuable resource to local winemakers, climatologists and historians alike. Today Chester treasures the information contained in it and keeps a printout of it in graph form in his office for easy reference. There were plenty of other activities to keep the winery busy in 1950 apart from vintage. A concrete loading platform was constructed; the winery was painted; near the currant shed a new tank stand was erected for a 2000-gallon tank; a new 30000-gallon concrete tank was built and the old currant patch was grubbed out. There was some replanting too: the Old Mataro was replaced with 4¼ acres of 1949 Grenache and 4½ acres of Palamino (two acres of Chenin Blanc were added in 1956). About 6000 gallons of wine was made for Emu and 5208 gallons for Penfolds at 5 shillings per gallon; 212 gallons of lees was sold to Hardy's and Tatachilla.[17]

The other side of the business was farming, and its history was also often recorded in d'Arry's shorthand: 'January — thatched haystack. June — wheat and barley planted — harvested by Neills; 3 ton hay'.[18] Details of workers and wages were noted, providing an excellent record of who was employed and when. Familiar McLaren Vale family names appear: 'S N King and Mrs King (May), John Bingapore and Bruce Carter, Dave Rayner' and others. Dave Rayner was one of generations of Rayners who worked for the Osborns. During the 1940s and 1950s vintages the pickers were mostly from the Aboriginal mission; 1950 was a landmark year when the pickers asked for, and received, an increase in wages from 26/- to 28/- per day. And, of course, the 1950 harvest was recorded:

SHIRAZ	11 TONS 8 CWT
MATARO	10 TONS 13 CWT
GRENACHE	21 TONS 6 CWT
CURRANTS	12 TONS 2 CWT
TOTAL	**121 TONS 9 CWT**

As we read through the diaries for the period from 1950 to 1957, we see a steady increase in yields by ten or more tonnes each year. At the same time, as d'Arry began to take charge of the running of the vineyard by upgrading its equipment, management changes were also made. On 1 July 1953 a partnership known as Bundarra Vineyards was established under which Frank and his three children were allocated percentage shares in the partnership and the company, F E Osborn & Sons. The shares were distributed proportionally, with Frank drawing four shares, Toni and Rowen one share each, and d'Arry two shares. Formalisation of this arrangement occurred when the company was registered in 1968. The partnership document described the business of Bundarra Vineyards as 'Vignerons and Winemakers'. The relationship between Bundarra Vineyards and F E Osborn & Sons was this: the partnership grew the grapes and the company (F E Osborn & Sons) made and then sold the wine (the partnership could not legally sell wine).

Nineteen fifty-four was a year of new beginnings for F E Osborn & Sons. d'Arry's diary recorded with delight that in January the foundations for his new cottage (now a staff office) were poured. He also noted that in May the family's long-term employees Mr and Mrs Norm King retired to Strathalbyn. The Kings had been with the Osborns since 1912; they gave 42 years service to the family. This is undoubtedly one of the hallmarks of an intergenerational family wine business where employees remain loyal to the company for decades. Many of the staff at d'Arenberg express this sense of being part of the family.

The balance sheets and profit and loss statements for 1954, the first year of operation under the new partnership, show the operating costs of the day. Wages were by far the highest cost at £3265; more than £2200 was spent on the purchase of wines and spirits; repairs, petrol, kerosene and power together came to £477, while seeds and fertilisers amounted to £244 — a far cry from today's costs!

The following year, 1955, brought a bumper crop of 219 tonnes of grapes producing 34 602 gallons of wine. A note next to his diary entry suggests d'Arry may have been a bit taken aback by this figure: 'total crop may be overestimated as this gives 158 gallons per acre'.[19] The result seems to have been exceptional at the time. The 1956 vintage began on 27 February and concluded on 11 April. In May they grubbed out currants and planted Palomino. d'Arry also noted that the well was pumping dry in five hours — it must have been a hot year. Again his diary provides a snapshot of the vintage, noting what was purchased from growers and what was being sold and to whom:

CROP:	SHIRAZ	55 TONS 6 CWT	BOUGHT IN:	SHIRAZ	3 TONS 14 CWT — S C THOM
	GRENACHE	41 TONS 8 CWT			5 TONS 9 CWT — E S DENNIS
	MATARO	6 TONS 15 CWT			9 TONS 3 CWT
	CURRANTS	7 TONS CWT		GORDO	6 TONS 14 CWT — F S CHADREL
	TOTAL		110 TONS 9 CWT		
	TOTAL CRUSHED		126 TONS 6 CWT		

WINE: EMU TOOK DELIVERY OF 5,150 GALLONS, ALEXANDER AND PATERSON TAKING PORT AND DRY RED. ANGOVES WOULD LIKE NO. 11, 1955 VINTAGE AT 5 SHILLINGS AND

6 PENCE, 9 PENCE UNDER OUR QUOTE. CHAFFEY BOUGHT 1,100 GALLONS SWEET WHITE, 1955, 1,100 GALLONS 1950; PORT 1,600 GALLONS AT 5 SHILLINGS AND 3 PENCE: 10,000 OF 1955 AND 1956 VINTAGES AT 5 SHILLINGS AND 9 PENCE AND REMAINDER (695 GALLONS) OF 1950 TAWNY.[20]

In a letter to his brother dated 19 November 1956, d'Arry informed Rowen that the vineyard was 'looking good'. The vines had been flowering for at least a fortnight 'doubtless due to the long cold winter' as they had had 'hardly any rain for 6 weeks'. Consequently the Shiraz was 'not likely to be anything startling', as the vines suffered heavily from 'wind and disease last year and snails this year'. More practical detail followed. He had used 500 pounds of bran for baits — possibly for snails. On the farming side, they had produced 800 bales of hay from the Big Paddock. There had been 'quite an improvement in wine sales' that year, 'though we haven't done much yet'. The remaining 1955 Burgundy had been fined and 'is acclaimed as one of the best we've made' by some of the experts. The Muscat and Grenache blend was also rather popular with the sweet sherry drinkers, he noted.[21]

Nineteen fifty-six was a significant year in Australian history — and especially in Australian wine history. It was the year of the Melbourne Olympic Games, and the year Barossa Pearl was launched. The Games, held from 22 November to 8 December, are remembered for many reasons, not least because it was the first time they were held in the southern hemisphere. The remoteness of Australia and two international crises accounted for the low number of participants: fewer than 3500 athletes from 67 countries attended. It was boycotted by teams from Egypt, Lebanon and Iraq in protest against the military assault on Egypt by Israeli,

British and French forces during the Sinai Crisis in October. The Netherlands, Spain, and Switzerland withdrew to protest the Soviet invasion of Hungary, also in October–November. East and West Germany for the first time competed as a single team. International politics played out on Australian soil, and 'Cold War tensions simmered and occasionally boiled over', as in the bloody underwater exchanges during a Soviet–Hungary water polo match.[22] In hosting the Games, Melburnians wanted to impress the world. What international visitors probably remembered best was six o'clock closing of pubs and the bizarre situation where 'half-full bottles of wine would be whisked from the table mid-way through an evening meal at a quality restaurant'.[23] South Australia was the last state to abolish this law when legislation introduced by Don Dunstan was passed in 1967.

Barossa Pearl, the new wine sensation of 1956, was created by Colin Gramp, who decided to produce the Australian equivalent of one of the sparkling 'perl' wines so popular in Germany. Having visited Germany and bought the necessary filtering and bottling equipment, he used pressure tanks to produce the 'fizz' generated by carbon dioxide. Gramp's wine was made from Tokay and Hunter River Riesling (Muscadelle and Sémillon) and presented in a bottle with a 'deliberate resemblance to the bulbous shape of a Perrier bottle'.[24] It was launched to coincide with the Olympics and was an immediate success. As Nicholas Faith points out, apart from its instant popularity, it was the first alternative for women drinkers to Rhinegold or the sweet sherry that 'had been their normal tipple' and it made wine drinking respectable for 'properly brought-up Australian women'. It was also one of the first wines promoted as being made using fruit from a single region. Barossa Pearl soon replaced the popular Rhinegold as the country's favourite non-fortified wine.[25]

The year 1956 is remembered less happily by Rowen, d'Arry and Toni as a turning point in their father's failing health marked by frequent and long periods of hospitalisation. In August he was ill with influenza and viral pneumonia. It was a worrying time for d'Arry, too. While his father was in hospital he received a phone call from the bank. John Jennings, a family friend, who was managing director of the ES&A Bank in Adelaide, asked d'Arry to come in for a chat. He was anxious to find out what was going to happen to the business. He said to d'Arry bluntly: 'It's no good you just making all this wine, you've got to get out there and sell it. I want you to do budgets, and I'll show you how to do them'. This news came as a bit of a shock to d'Arry at the time, but he now reflects:

> *It was the best thing we ever did and it's why the business is so successful today. If you do budgets and you're strong enough to stick to them, you've got a fair chance of making it. You ought to see our budgets now: they're quite complex...*[26]

It was an important lesson: d'Arry now had a plan and budget to follow.

The following year, 1957, d'Arry's diary listed his father's worsening health problems: 'May, glaucoma, bronchitis. In hospital from 24 June (pneumonia).'[27] Frank Osborn spent his final days at the Southern Districts War Memorial Hospital and passed away on 3 August 1957. After many years of illness, his death couldn't have been unexpected. His obituary in the *Australian Brewing and Wine Journal* characterised him first as a respected pioneering vigneron of the district:

His whole career has been described as an example of a modest grapegrowing and winemaking business that has maintained a sturdily independent existence. In recent years, though suffering from much ill-health, Mr Osborn continued to show this plucky spirit to the end.[28]

Mr Osborn was prominent in Legacy Club work, particularly in helping organise meat supplies for the Legacy boys and girls' camps at Clarendon. In the RSL he was foundation chairman of McLaren Vale sub-branch in 1919–20, and occupied the chair again later for two terms. He was a member of the District Council of Noarlunga from 1925 to 1930. Mr Osborn left two sons — Rowen, in the Australian diplomatic service in Holland; and d'Arenberg (Darry) [sic] who is continuing the vineyard and winery business in partnership with his brother and their sister, Antoinette, who is in London. Mrs Osborn died many years ago.[29]

Although this obituary has only recently come to light, it is gratifying to his children to know that their father's contribution to the community was so highly regarded. As suggested, his shares in the business partnership were taken over by the three children, with d'Arry purchasing a portion of the other partners' allocations. This arrangement has remained in place since 1957.

Fertile ground for change

From the mid to late 1950s d'Arry had quietly observed that Australian attitudes towards wine were slowly changing.[30] The wine-drinking population at large was

still unsophisticated, so in 1955 the Australian Wine Board decided to embark on a national wine advertising campaign, which ran from August 1955 to July 1956.[31] The campaign was funded by a grape levy of six shillings per tonne. A Wine Information Centre was established in Sydney; 500 000 information booklets on wine were distributed throughout Australia and advertisements ran in the popular weekly magazines. The entire campaign, which focused on table wines, cost £39 000. By the time it was reviewed in 1960, a rapid increase in wine consumption was evident.[32]

It has been argued that the increase in consumption of table wine came about because of the various waves of postwar European migrants and their 'dietary and culinary' influence on the largely white Anglo-Saxon population — that is, that the population acquired a taste for wine by 'rubbing shoulders with wine drinkers' from other countries. In reality, the story appears to be more nuanced than this. Anecdotal evidence suggests that the Greek, Italian and Yugoslav migrants preferred to drink beer in public, and that their tastes in wine ran to the wine they produced themselves in their own garages, rather than the wines made by big Australian companies such as Penfolds or Lindeman's. As important as an increasingly multicultural Australia was, overseas travel was equally if not more responsible for the new trend of wine drinking. Much like their parents a generation before them, large numbers of 18 to 35 year olds enthusiastically left Australia's shores to travel overseas to London and Europe. Australia's youth wanted to experience European culture and taste French, Italian and German wines for themselves. They did not necessarily want to buy Australian wine from the Australian Wine Centre in Soho, London, either, as something of a cultural cringe existed when it came to expatriate Aussies buying Australian wine.[33] However, when many of these intrepid travellers returned to Australia they wanted to continue drinking wine with their meals.

But there is more to it than that. Two other factors must be remembered here: the first is the removal of beer rationing; the second is the emergence of an active wine press. The end of beer rationing was disastrous for the wine market because the consumption of fortified wine declined drastically. However, when Barossa Pearl was launched in 1956 it stormed the market and introduced 'countless thousands of Australians to wine' at a time when wine consumption had slipped to 5.8 litres per head. Finally, by the late 1950s and early 1960s a more affluent Australian population wanted to read and be educated about Australian table wine: this in turn boosted its popularity, increased consumption and eventually changed the making and marketing of Australian wine.

CHAPTER 5

The story behind the d'Arenberg stripe

WHEN FRANK OSBORN WAS ALIVE HE HAD NO DESIRE TO MAKE TABLE WINE and bottle it.[1] Although it was becoming fashionable and increasingly evident that it was economically necessary to do so, it meant expanding the business to include cellar door sales and, to a certain extent, managing the marketing and distribution of the wine. Frank was too ill to take on these extra responsibilities.

By the late 1950s, after having worked in the winery for 16 years, two of them in his own right as manager and winemaker, d'Arry could see the way the industry and the market were changing. He recognised the need to expand the winery and dreamed of moving from producing bulk wines to creating a table wine with his own label. After his father died he made a conscious decision to work towards this goal, taking the next step by establishing an individual label for Osborn wines. In 1958 he joined the South Australian Wine and Brandy Producers' Association, an organisation he continues to be associated with. This was a pragmatic move. It was the breweries rather than the hoteliers who purchased wine from the wine companies and effectively controlled the retail price, and the breweries refused to buy from any winemaker who was not a member of the Wine and Brandy Producers' Association.[2] d'Arry also joined the association so he could get to know the industry and the people better. He wanted to go to regular meetings and functions; he wanted and needed to learn about managing a winery.[3] Although he himself would never express it in these terms, the boy who had left school at 16 was now, at age 32, successfully managing his own small and growing business.

d'Arry Osborn: making wine by the seat of his pants

d'Arry's decision to enter the wine market as a producer of his own wines rather than of bulk wines for large distributors and wine companies occurred at a pivotal time. Just as his father had begun to produce bottled wine in 1928 when the overseas market was expanding rapidly, d'Arry was embarking on producing his own label when the Australian domestic wine market was beginning to re-establish itself. The bottling, labelling and marketing of wine by its producers was a development that would have a profound significance on the immediate future of the wine industry in the postwar era. Wine historian John Beeston perceives the 'stirrings for change' in McLaren Vale. 'Some small makers such as Osborn were even thinking of their own label…'[4] d'Arry could read the market: he was neither leading the industry nor lagging behind it.

Although a general interest in wine drinking was increasing in Australia in the late 1950s, it was an industry influenced by fashion and price — recurring themes through the history of the wine industry. During the Second World War when beer was scarce, wine became more popular, consumption increasing from

14.5 million litres in 1939 to 37 million litres by 1944.[5] By the 1950s, while Leo Buring was marketing the sweet lighter wine style of Rhinegold, Ron Haselgrove of Angoves was beginning to think the Australian claret style would soon make an impact on the national palate. At Penfolds the young Jeffrey Penfold Hyland also believed red table wine had a commercial future in Australia and sent their young winemaker Max Schubert to study winemaking in France. Max ultimately made his name with the famous Grange Hermitage, but that subject requires a book in its own right. As we have seen, however, the removal of beer rationing and the liberalisation of the licensing laws as a result of a royal commission saw another decline in wine consumption. For those who were not wine drinkers, the drink of the 1950s was beer or scotch for men and a little sweet sherry for women.[6]

By 1960 the tide was turning, the attitude to Australian dry red wine was changing and Penfolds became 'masters of what would be called Australia's cellar style dry reds'.[7] The new generation of baby-boomers began to be influenced by European culture, partly through postwar immigration. The decade also ushered in years of high employment levels and the growth of a relatively affluent middle class whose interest in wine was served by an explosion of wine- and food-related clubs that sprang up in every suburb and country town. Or, as David Dunstan prefers, an emergent circle of connoisseurs 'quickly discovered that elitism had its rewards in convivial company and insider access to superior product. Connoisseurs traded information and banded together in wine and food societies to learn more'.[8] During the 1950s and early 1960s men who were interested in food and wine joined the local Bacchus Club or the Beefsteak and Burgundy Club; for women it was the Chicken and Chablis Club. Additionally, eating out at restaurants, mainly

Italian, became the fashion, and this too was a gift for the wine industry. Barossa Pearl swamped the restaurant market and 'subsidised the minuscule yet growing quantities of dry reds which were just beginning to find favour with an increasing number of younger sophisticated consumers'.[9] It was against this backdrop that F E Osborn & Sons took steps to create the d'Arenberg label.

Creating the d'Arenberg label

Wine production at Bundarra in 1957 saw incremental increases on the 1956 level: 146 tonnes was picked and 61 tonnes purchased, making a total of 207 tonnes crushed. That year wine was sold to Emu Wine Company, Angoves and Ben Chaffey at Coriole with some additional customers, notably their neighbours the Kay brothers, of Amery, who took 1650 gallons of Sweet White at 9 shillings and sixpence per gallon. Chaffey paid 8 shillings and 9 pence for Gordo, 5 shillings and 6 pence for Doradilla and 5 shillings and 3 pence for Grenache/Gordo.[10] d'Arry also found that enquiries for his red wine in particular were coming in from 'all over the place' and wrote to Rowen that they must try to increase production.[11] In early December d'Arry was probably relieved to record that Ben Chaffey was taking the 1300 gallons of Dry White and the remainder of the Sweet White the following year. Nineteen fifty-eight saw an even greater increase of wine produced and grapes purchased: a total of 275 tonnes crushed. A note on the cellar door trade, not previously mentioned in his diary, appeared for the first time that year. Burgundy, Sweet White, Dry White, Tawny Port, Dry Red and Sweet Red were all sold by the gallon to Vintage Cellars, while the remaining wine was sold to their usual list of wine merchants. d'Arry could inform Rowen, who was then working as Second Secretary at the Australian Embassy in The Hague, that the total wine made was approximately 39 000 gallons. He made both Dry Red and Sweet Red: 'the quality', he wrote, 'was extra good and the best block was the young Grenache where we harvested 40 tons from 8 acres'. Further good news was that the cellars were 'full to the brim'.[12]

Before launching their own label, Osborn wines were labelled as non-vintage and sold under generic names — Claret, Burgundy, Moselle, Hock, Chablis and so on. Of the 1958 vintage, d'Arry noted that the demand for Dry Red was 'good'; that the wines 'seem a bit acid but the colour was good'; and that he would test at about 23.5 per cent to 25 per cent.[13] Technical details were also conveyed to his brother, who of course was keen to hear the news.

WINE: 5,000 SR (Sweet Red) was brought up to desired strength [on] 27.5.58, 34% and 26% with Baume 4.5° and 6.5° respectively. SO² 80 ppm and 320 ppm also respectively. The high sulphur contact in the low strength has knocked the colour a bit but they are both extra good on the palate.

CAR: F J Holden traded in on new F E Holden plus £320.[14]

Like his father, d'Arry loved his cars.

The d'Arenburgundy

As production increased, it became clear that more land was required. In August 1958 their neighbour Rex Spong offered to sell a portion of Section 128, Hundred of Willunga, at £150 per acre or £12 000 in total. An earlier owner of this land, Frederick Shipster, had planted it with vines and an orchard in 1916. d'Arry claimed he would not spend this amount per acre, but on 20 September he paid a deposit of £491 5s 0d for 32¾ acres, with the balance due on 20 November 1958. In due course this additional land was cleared and progressively planted with vines.

The arrival of Pauline and d'Arry's first child, a daughter, on 22 July 1959, was cause for great celebration in McLaren Vale. d'Arry was, of course, well known in wine circles, so it is not a surprise to see this event reported in the *Australian Brewing and Wine Journal*: 'Mr and Mrs d'Arry Osborn, of Bundarra Vineyard, McLaren Vale, have been receiving felicitations on the birth of their first child, Jacqueline Helena, on July 22, at Calvary Hospital, North Adelaide'[15] — Jacqueline after a friend of Pauline's, and Helena after d'Arry's mother. One month later the *Journal* featured another snippet about the Osborn family:

Mr F d'Arenberg Osborn, as principal of F E Osborn & Sons, McLaren Vale, was elected as a new member of the Winemakers' Association of South Australia at the association meeting on August 21. Mr Osborn conducts Bundarra Vineyard and its winery, founded by his father, the late Mr Francis E Osborn, 47 years ago.[16]

The article is accompanied by a photograph of a smiling d'Arry.

With the quality and production capacity of Bundarra wines increasing each year, d'Arry and Pauline talked about creating an individual label. It was a subject close to d'Arry's heart. In the early months of 1959 they began to design the new label. 'I'd always wanted my own label and I thought I'd call it d'Arenberg'.[17] The inspiration for the name is clear; it was to be named after Frances Helena d'Arenberg, the mother he never knew, but it was his own name too. As he told historian Susan Marsden, 'Of course I was d'Arenberg, everybody called me "d'Arenberg" or "d'Arry" for short, and so d'Arenberg seemed a good name for wine'.[18] d'Arry had helped his friend and neighbour Ben Chaffey set up and run a new winery and called it Seaview; the two became great friends. When he told Chaffey he was launching a label, Chaffey 'urged him to make it distinctive'. He 'told me I needed to get something like that [the Seaview label] and stick to it, so that people would remember it', d'Arry recalls.[19]

At a meeting of the Wine and Brandy Producers' Association, he discussed this idea with Jeffrey Penfold Hyland, then president of the association. d'Arry told him he was thinking of calling the new label 'd'Arenburgundy'. When Penfold Hyland replied that 'd'Arenberg Burgundy' sounded all right but that 'd'Arenburgundy' would be 'rubbished a bit', d'Arry was not put off.[20] The name 'd'Arenburgundy' obviously lingered in his mind, as it reappeared a few years later. The d'Arenberg label, with its distinctive red stripe, was introduced for the 1959 vintage. The wine was a combination of Shiraz and Grenache, sold as Burgundy — the same wine he and his father had been making for decades.

Wine writer Nicholas Faith, who describes d'Arry as 'a man of great gentleness and passion, and no mean winemaker', relates that the young d'Arry was greatly

helped in his first vintage by Cuthbert Thornborough Kay (known as Cud) of Kay Brothers, a much-loved winemaker in McLaren Vale. 'On one occasion d'Arry took him two buckets of his unfermented juice and returned with two buckets of Cud's wine. He then kick-started the fermentation of his vats in a primitive but effective fashion.'[21]

The combination of Grenache and Shiraz has remained one of d'Arenberg's flagship wines. However, when first produced, d'Arry bottled the wine in a Burgundy bottle, signifying that it was a wine in a softer style. The 'd'Arenberg' label was acknowledged for the first time in the wine press on 21 August 1961. The *Australian Wine, Brewing and Spirit Review* announced:

Friends of Mr F d'A Osborn of Bundarra Vineyards, McLaren Vale, S.A., have been interested to observe a bottling of Burgundy from this winery circulating among sundry friends and other 'initiates'. It is the first time a printed-label bottling has been put out by F E Osborn & Sons, and they still continue as essentially bulk suppliers. The wine is labelled as 'd'Arenberg Burgundy', bringing in a family name which is the maker's second Christian name, usually contracted to d'Arry. The crest on the label has beneath it the Latin motto, Vinum Vita Est, *meaning Wine is Life. It is a 1960 Shiraz of delightful and distinctive character.*[22]

According to a report of the 22 February 1963 McLaren Vale Bacchus Club dinner that appeared in the March *Australian Wine, Brewing and Spirit Review*, 70 members met that evening and the club's president, Mr Ken Maxwell, introduced a series of speakers at the various stages of the meal. The club's cellarmaster,

Mr John Kilgour, who spoke on the wines, described the 'd'Arenburgundy' as a 'robust vigorous dry red'.[23] d'Arry seems to have won naming rights on this occasion.

Behind the label

d'Arry had always envisaged including a stripe on his label. His inspirations were the diagonal blue stripe of the Houghton's wine label, which he especially liked, and happy memories of his school days at Prince Alfred College, where he wore the crimson-and-white striped school tie. His great friend Don Allnut (Nutty) worked for Rupert Murdoch as a designer, eventually heading their art department. Don had attended the opposition school, St Peter's Church of England, whose emblem is blue and white. When d'Arry asked him to design a label with a red stripe on it, Don sent him down to the public library to find a crest. The librarian's research revealed that there had long been a d'Arenberg heraldic crest, which included a tangerine stripe, the Bar Sinister. This crest was probably found in J B Rietstap's *General Armorial*.[24] How they acquired a copy of the d'Arenberg coat of arms is a mystery, as these were the days before photocopying. Nevertheless, Don Allnut designed a label — but with a tangerine stripe. As d'Arry recalls, his exasperated response to Don was: 'It's red wine, not bloody tangerine, you Saints boy!' The story remained a joke between the two friends for years.

The launch of the new wine under the resplendent new label — including the red stripe — was, we are told, 'both small and humble' and involved 'half-gallon flagons and a small quantity of table wines'.[25]

At the time d'Arry did not consider the fact that the label on Mumm champagne also had a red stripe, albeit at that time paler and broader — these days, d'Arry believes, the colour has been darkened. Having modelled the d'Arenberg label on the d'Arenberg coat of arms, d'Arry thought no more about it for more than 10 years. Names and labels continued to be created: in 1960, for example, d'Arry came up with the Antoinette Port and the Rowen Muscat. Together with the d'Arenberg Burgundy, the three siblings now each had their own label, although the Rowen Muscat never appeared.[26]

Years of growth

In a recent interview for a *WBM: Australia's Wine Business Magazine* feature on father-and-son winemakers, d'Arry joked that when he first started, 'I made wine by the seat of my pants'. Luckily he had a natural ability and understood the vineyard. Before Chester was born, in the late 1950s, the McLaren Vale Wine Co-operative invited guest speakers to talk about winemaking. They 'pulled our wines to bits to show us how much better they could be'. At this stage, of course, there were only about ten wineries in McLaren Vale. d'Arry recalls that on one such occasion, Geoff Merrill asked him, '"I hear you've started vintage. What was the pH and titratable acidity?" I said, "I don't know." He said, "How could you start picking if you didn't know that?" I said, "Well, the grapes and pips were brown and the leaves were coming off the vines and they tasted ripe to me".'[27] Fifty years later this is how Chester decides when to pick and make wine too.

During these exciting years of expansion when the new venture of selling wine under their own label took off, new storage tanks and other equipment were needed. In 1959 d'Arry purchased a 46 000-litre concrete tank, bringing the total tank storage to 86 000 litres. The following year four more five-tonne concrete fermenters were built along with a shed to house them. During 1961 a 26 300-litre wooden vat was purchased from Leo Buring and, to everyone's great joy, the nineteenth-century hydraulic 'Coq' basket press was acquired from Yalumba and installed at d'Arenberg. At the same time they bought three more wooden vats, raising the storage capacity to 191 200 litres.[28] When the distinctive d'Arenberg label with its red stripe was introduced in 1960, d'Arry planted the first Cabernet Sauvignon vines. These were among the first to be planted in McLaren Vale. Glen McWilliam planted some at Hanwood near Griffith; some were planted at Oxford Landing on the Murray River, and another vineyard was established high above Pewsey Vale.[29] Further plantings of this variety and Shiraz helped develop the vineyard to 150 acres. Blends of these varieties were used to make the Claret and Burgundy styles. Osborn's 1961 vintage was drastically reduced because of a prolonged drought in South Australia.

d'Arry estimated that the yield for his 1962 vintage would be almost double that of 1961 — they picked about 110 tonnes and bought in around 200 tonnes of grapes.[30] From the first, d'Arry's diary had noted the nationalities of the pickers they hired during vintage. Initially they had been Aboriginal workers, but from 1959 they also employed Dutch and Greek migrants. The work was intense: at one stage they crushed 50 tonnes in three days, making full use of all fermenting space. d'Arry estimated that, if pushed, they could press five tanks a day and still handle incoming loads.[31] Work completed around the vineyard in 1962 included building a new cellar, installing a new wine pump and planting four acres of Spongs Flat purchased in 1958 (Lot 128). After attending a meeting of the Wine and Brandy Producers' Association in October 1962, d'Arry wrote: 'There is concern about over-production of wine and limited ability of wineries to handle another big vintage. 40,000 tons more than ever before processed last year. Emu look like easing off in their buying too'.[32]

This was indeed a portent of things to come. Although public awareness of table wine was growing all the time, in its annual report the Australian Wine Board made two important points: that the 1962 vintage was by far the biggest in the history of the Australian wine industry; and that further large vintages could prove to be an embarrassment as the industry could not guarantee to process all available crops.[33] The Australian economy was not in good shape at this time. The balance of payments led to a severe credit squeeze, unemployment jumped from 2 to 3 per cent, and in the federal election Robert Menzies' Liberal Party was returned by the narrowest of margins. This in turn led to a slump in grape prices. The 1960s saw exports from the McLaren Vale fall into the doldrums.[34] Yet history repeats itself and the wine industry, like other Australian industries, has frequently oscillated between shortage and surplus.

From 1961 the Emu Wine Company began to limit purchases from McLaren Vale, although it bought the nearby Tatachilla for £330 000 in 1962. Rising costs, growing competition from European and British wines, reduced custom preferences and Britain's possible entry into the European Economic Community (EEC), or Common Market, were all cited as reasons for the merger. Both companies had headquarters in London and it was decided to amalgamate their warehouse facilities, although the two South Australian vineyards were to continue to operate separately.[35] Tatachilla was soon closed down. In 1963 d'Arry recorded in his diary: 'Tatachilla men are being paid off. Harvey Eatts taken on [at Bundarra] after 17 years at Tatachilla as cellar man and Cyril McGavin taken on after 13 years in vineyard at Tatachilla and moved into cottage January'.[36]

Nineteen sixty-two was an important year for the Australian wine industry. Most importantly for the Osborn family, Chester d'Arenberg Osborn was born. The *Australian Wine, Brewing and Spirit Review* announced:

> *… births in the wine industry in S.A. recently have been the cause of rejoicing. Mr and Mrs d'Arry Osborn of McLaren Vale, had their second child, a son, Chester d'Arenberg, on July 1, hailed by d'Arry as a good start to the financial year, and boasting the unusual length of 22 inches. D'Arry and Pauline Osborn now have a boy and a girl (Jacqueline).*[37]

The year has two more claims to wine fame: it marked the establishment of the Jimmy Watson Memorial Trophy; and Len Evans began his quest to educate Australians about table wine by publishing his first regular column in *The Bulletin*. Jimmy Watson's Wine Bar had been launched in Lygon Street, Carlton, in 1935 and became something of an institution, serving wine Watson bottled himself as well as some aged vintages for his discerning customers. The business flourished, especially after 1945, as his entry in *The Australian Dictionary of Biography* notes. What made his wine bar different was not just that he welcomed international

visitors, but that he made women comfortable in the wine bar environment. Wine bars at the time generally had the reputation of being seedy, undesirable places. Watson was an independent operator with no ties to wine companies and he would not sell wine by the flagon. By the 1960s, it is said, many tourists to Victoria thought Watson's premises were a more important landmark than the Melbourne Town Hall.[38] Watson, who had suffered from diabetes for several years, died of a coronary occlusion in February 1962. Several hundred people attended his funeral and fellow traders lined both sides of Lygon Street. His friends instituted the Jimmy Watson Memorial Trophy at the annual Royal Melbourne Wine Show for the best one-year-old red, a style of wine that he had stocked for his customers to buy and cellar.[39] The inaugural winner was Stonyfell Wines.[40]

Wine writing and publishing, as David Dunstan reminds us, did not just start in the postwar era but it did increase in volume from that time. English journalist-cum-winemaker Walter James published *Barrel and Book* in 1949, and went on to publish more than half a dozen 'witty erudite books' on wine over a 30-year period.[41] James's books were best-sellers and helped sow the seeds of appreciation for wine and food that were to bloom in the 1960s.[42] Instituted in 1962, *The Bulletin*'s 'Cellarmaster' column was the first regular wine column in Australian newspapers. It was written by the then 30-year-old 'Welsh immigrant with a golden tongue', Len Evans. Until succeeded by Dan Murphy, he wrote the Cellarmaster column 'with a verve and wit hardly ever seen in the more serious wine writing of the present time' and helped those interested in it acquire expertise in wine.[43] Evans steered drinkers away from fortified wines and towards great Australian and international table wines. Although some in the trade 'chose to see Evans as an opportunist, a mere surfer on the wave of wine's growing popularity', Charles Gent believes it would be difficult to imagine the change in public attitudes without his stamp.[44] Today it is an essential ingredient of success for winemakers and their wines to be reviewed in the numerous wine columns of the popular and wine press. Journalists who occasionally wrote about wine in this decade were Frank Doherty, John Hetherington and Keith Dunstan.

Despite a relatively small vintage Australia-wide in 1963, the bumper vintage of 1962 led to the subsequent oversupply of wine grapes. In 1964 the Australian Wine Board reported that the main surplus of grapes was in South Australia. This was hardly a surprise as South Australia was the major producer of Australian wine. A group of growers formed a new cooperative company to handle the surplus. Despite beginning production very late in the vintage, the Berri Wine Co-operative handled more than 1600 tonnes of grapes.

The years 1963 and 1964 were slow for F E Osborn & Sons. In 1963 d'Arry picked only 100 tonnes and bought in as much as possible from growers. Sales the following year were also very slow. In 1964 the first tasting room was built at d'Arenberg, extensions were made to the cellar and house, and five more wooden vats were purchased from Tatachilla, raising total storage volume to 322 700 litres. Angoves bought 20 400 gallons; d'Arry had '49 000 [gallons] on offer but nobody buying very much'.[45] He entered four Dry Reds, one Dry White and one Muscat in the Adelaide wine show — no medals, but '13.5 points out of 20, generally 25th out of 40 entries'. We can sense the note of pride in this comment.[46]

Already a member of the South Australian Wine and Brandy Producers' Association, in 1964 d'Arry became an executive member and also a delegate to the

Federal Wine and Brandy Producers' Council, which became the Australian Wine and Brandy Association with d'Arry as its executive treasurer. He also stood on the association as a small producer. At the suggestion of Ian Seppelt, he joined the Adelaide Chamber of Commerce in 1965; he served on the ACC council for 20 years.

Wine sales began to pick up in 1965, a year that saw the acquisition of several important new pieces of equipment. Of great pride to d'Arry, a Coldstream refrigeration unit was one of the latest technologies adopted. The refrigeration system, pioneered by Colin Gramp in his production of Barossa Pearl, was installed to cool fermenters, eliminating the need for cool bore water. Also purchased was the largest oval barrel ever installed in the southern hemisphere, holding 37 300 litres. The second-hand unit had been imported from the United States. At the same time two wooden vats were acquired, bringing storage volume to 423 000 litres. (Only two years later, in 1968, five more wooden vats were purchased, once again increasing the total storage volume, this time to nearly 600 000 litres.)

For the first time in some years, in 1965 new buyers appeared in the office records. As well as selling to Lindeman's and Wynn's, Buring & Sobels were buying wine for the Bistro Steak House in Gilbert Place, Adelaide. d'Arry excitedly records that the Bistro Steak House 'sold by carafe 9 shillings, ½ carafe 4 shillings and six pence, and by the glass for 1 shilling and six pence. Average of 400 meals per day; best consumption 120 flagons on a Saturday'. These were statistics to ponder, as Buring & Sobels bought the bulk wine at 8 shillings per gallon. We can almost hear d'Arry's mental calculations of how much they might make if they sold direct to the Bistro Steak House. At this stage, F E Osborn & Sons did not distribute its own wine, still selling most of it as bulk wine. Experimenting with labelling and marketing under the d'Arenberg brand was still in its early stages. In James Halliday's estimation, however, while there was a groundswell of opinion seeking change to the status quo of wine sales and distribution, it met with formidable opposition in the form of the 'unholy alliance between the hoteliers, their brewery masters, and the temperance league'. Shifts in the methods of selling and consuming wine came 'painfully slowly'. One catalyst was the gradual appearance of 'continental-style grocers' with some form of liquor licence. Italian restaurants encouraged patrons to bring their own wine; some sold it illegally (the Italian Waiters Club in Melbourne comes to mind). Australians who had travelled overseas to Europe, and European immigrants, expected to be able to buy and consume wine in restaurants in public.[47] Change occurred slowly in Australia.

The Baileys of Glenrowen challenge the Bundarra name

As a result of the changes made to the company structure in 1953, Bundarra Vineyards was trading as F E Osborn & Sons. The Osborns had always known that the Bailey family of Glenrowen had a well-established winery of the same name in central Victoria. Frank, who had chosen the name 'Bundarra' in 1912, apparently had neither the desire nor the will to change it. Whether consciously or unconsciously, d'Arry also chose to ignore this aspect of his family business. It was probably something of a surprise, therefore, when the family received a letter from the Bailey brothers in February 1965 informing F E Osborn & Sons that they had applied for trademark protection. After family consultation d'Arry, who was the largest shareholder in the business, decided he was 'prepared to let the name go', but at a cost to the Baileys. No-one had any suggestion for an alternative Aboriginal name. When d'Arry thought about this a little further, he remembered that the issue had cropped up in the past. Essentially, it was all right to use the name 'Bundarra' but not to sell wine under that name. d'Arry spoke on the phone to fellow winemaker Alan Bailey about the matter. When he explained he'd just had new labels produced, Alan offered to pay the cost of them by way of compensation.[48] In this way the issue was resolved to everyone's satisfaction. By mutual agreement, the use of the name 'Bundarra' for the property effectively ceased and the partnership established in 1953 and formerly known as Bundarra Vineyards was renamed F E Osborn & Sons.

This was not the last such battle they would have to fight.

Winning wines

With issues of the company name resolved, d'Arry was heartened by the increase in wine sales in the second half of the 1960s. More importantly, d'Arenberg-labelled wines were now winning prizes at wine shows. In July 1966, while the nation was coming to grips with the change in currency from pounds, shillings and pence to dollars and cents, d'Arry joined the Executive Board of the South Australian Wine and Brandy Producers' Association and was elected as a delegate to the Federal

Wine and Brandy Producers' Council. He also sold bottled wine to the Naval and Military Club for the first time — in this case the 1963 Burgundy — and 12 dozen of the 1964 Cabernet Shiraz to the Adelaide Bacchus Club for binning. This wine was sold direct to the customer rather than through a distributor or hotel chain. The wine market was improving, as was the quality of his wines. He had the pleasure of informing Rowen, who was then working as a Counsellor at the Australian High Commission in London,[49] that the vineyard 'looks better than it has for years. Rains have come along nicely in the spring and cultivation and pruning was all done nice and early'.[50] The following year more of Spong's land was cleared and planted, and all roads on the property were remade with limestone from the Spong quarry. Wine prices were rising quickly; Seppelts, to whom they were still selling in bulk, wanted 10 000 gallons of the 1968 vintage at $2 per gallon and bottled wines were selling for up to $20 per dozen. d'Arry acknowledged in 1966 that a shortage in reds was likely to continue for two to three years, by which time he hoped to establish agents in other states, which in due course he did.[51]

The prediction of a wine shortage did not worry F E Osborn & Sons; they had plenty of dry red in their cellars, and an article in the Cellarmaster column of *The Bulletin* in February 1967 accelerated their orders, which were now coming in from all quarters — from Hobart, Perth, Brisbane, Sydney and Melbourne. In one week d'Arry recorded '300 dozen sent away'. In 1967 his Dry Red Claret won a silver medal at the South Australian wine show. By April 1968 d'Arry had established agents in Melbourne, G H Adams Pty Ltd of West Melbourne, who at the time placed wine in 52 of the best hotels and restaurants in Melbourne. By July they had d'Arenberg wines in 70 Melbourne outlets; in August they won two silver and one bronze medal at the Melbourne Wine Show. Doug Collett was engaged to assist with the business side of the organisation to allow d'Arry time to concentrate on winemaking. He finally organised labels for his Claret, Tawny Port, Amontillado Dry Sherry and Vintage Port.

With the Baileys' claim on the 'Bundarra' name still ringing in their ears, the Osborn businesses were formalised. On 4 November 1968 F E Osborn & Sons Pty Ltd was registered as a proprietary company and d'Arenberg Wines Pty Ltd was also registered. Fifty-one per cent of this company was owned by F E Osborn & Sons Pty Ltd, 49 per cent by Doug Collett's company, Olinga Pty Ltd. Incorporation of the name coincided with an aggressive campaign to market the d'Arenberg label. Until 1985 Osborn Vineyards grew the grapes, F E Osborn & Sons Pty Ltd bought the grapes and made the wine, which was bottled and marketed by d'Arenberg Wines Pty Ltd. However, F E Osborn & Sons actually retained ownership of the wine even when it was in bottles owned by d'Arenberg Wines Pty Ltd. F E Osborn & Sons owned the name d'Arenberg and the red stripe.

The Jimmy Watson Trophy

Only one month after Neil Armstrong's historic walk on the moon, in August 1969, Toni, Rowen and d'Arry Osborn and families were themselves walking on air when d'Arenberg Wines won the prized Jimmy Watson Memorial Trophy for the best 1968 vintage Claret or Burgundy. The Trophy was won for the 1968 Cabernet Sauvignon. They also won two gold, two silver and five bronze at the Melbourne

Wine Show. In June, however, pressure of work and financial worries combined to drive d'Arry to a state of exhaustion and elevated blood pressure, although this soon settled, as he conveyed to Rowen in a letter on 22 August, only days after the announcement of the Jimmy Watson Trophy win. A bottling line was installed at the winery, allowing d'Arenberg to bottle its own wine on site. The first stage of a new bottling shed and a new port shed were constructed in 1969 and the purchase of a further six wooden vats brought the total volume of wine storage to 637 000 litres. Wine sales continued to increase and in 1970 they again purchased almost double the tonnage they produced, along with an additional two stainless steel tanks and two wooden vats, raising storage volume to 694 600 litres. As well, in 1970 they entered into a very successful joint distribution venture with another intergenerational family-owned winery, the central Victorian Chateau Tahbilk. They completed the second stage of the bottling shed in 1971, but perhaps the most gratifying event of the year was the awarding of the A C Kelly Trophy at the Royal Adelaide Show to the d'Arenberg 1967 Burgundy. The 1970s were shaping up well for d'Arenberg Wines.

The Bushing Festival

One of the most successful ventures of the 1970s for the entire McLaren Vale winemaking district was the establishment of the annual Bushing Festival. The inaugural festival took place in 1973. The committee behind the initiative included well-known winemakers Colin Kay, James Ingoldby, Alex Johnston and d'Arry

Osborn; viticulturist David Hardy; hotelier Michael Vandeleur; and company directors Noel Davey and Morris Kearney. Beryl Davey was the festival secretary. John Williamson, of Williamson & Associates, TV journalist Anthony Brooks and solicitor Neil Hume completed the committee.

As the program explains, the festival's name had an ancient derivation:

Long before King Henry the Seventh first regulated ale-houses by Act of Parliament, setting up provisions for 'bush houses' at village fairs so that ale and wine could be sold without licence, the 'bush' had been used as a sign that good things were available within.

Celebrating nearly 150 years of winemaking history in McLaren Vale and recognising that there were greater things to come were the underlying themes of the festival. Its two main aims were to promote the sale of wines and to promote the McLaren Vale region as one of the most important winemaking regions in Australia, thereby increasing both regional and national tourism. The event was timed to celebrate the first release of their new wines and the people who made them. The 10-day festival included wine tours, tastings, spectacular displays, feasting and dancing. A 'Bushing King and Queen' were elected to preside over the activities and celebrations. The first Bushing Festival was a hugely successful event, and the lessons of the early festivals were drawn on to ensure the ongoing success of subsequent festivals. The popular wine critic and writer Len Evans attended the second Bushing Festival and wrote to d'Arry in early November 1974 of his impressions. He commended the Bushing Ball and described the

Elizabethan feast as 'probably the greatest visual spectacle' he had seen in catering events in Australia.[52] Evans had pioneered the Elizabethan feast in New South Wales so could offer some valuable suggestions for improvements for the following year's festival.

In 1976, d'Arry acted as festival president and the event was opened by the South Australian Premier, Don Dunstan. The annual festival grew in popularity and importance as a regional tourist attraction. Wine sales increased for all the winemakers who took part, and it soon became a pivotal wine event of the year. Today both the Bushing Festival and the Sea and Vines Festival continue to be celebrated annually in McLaren Vale.

Prince Erik and the d'Arenberg dispute

If the Baileys' letter of claim to the Bundarra name had surprised the Osborn family in 1965, the letter from Prince Erik, Duke d'Arenberg, a member of the European d'Arenberg family, that arrived in 1974 must surely have shocked them more. Prince Erik had come across a bottle of d'Arenberg wine, heard of the family in Australia and wrote to insist they cease using the d'Arenberg name. We know that d'Arry chose the name d'Arenberg to honour his mother, and to use his own given name, but in truth the Osborn family knew little about the d'Arenberg family origins. What they did know was largely hearsay, but after serious investigation they found some surprising family history. Here is what they discovered.

115

The ducal house of Arenberg was prominent in Europe for hundreds of years, reaching its zenith in the seventeenth and eighteenth centuries. Much material documenting the family history is held in the family archives at Enghien in Belgium, in the General Archives of the Kingdom of Brussels and by the Arenberg Foundation in Essen, Germany. Books have been published about the family; a four-volume series, in German, was issued in 1990. References to a d'Arenberg having fought with Napoleon's armies in Russia, and to a d'Arenberg who had been forced into exile after having killed a man in a duel, appear in one volume. There is separate evidence to show that the son of Ignatius, Count d'Arenberg, and his wife Rosina d'Arles, a John George d'Arenberg, was born at Mannheim in 1768. It is John George who is said to have fled to Ireland and adopted the name Abeltshauser. There is also evidence that an Ignatius George Abeltshauser (Helena's grandfather) was born in Strasbourg in 1805. Until the 1970s the various European d'Arenberg families were unaware of any Australian branch of the family.

The story of Helen Frances Osborn (née Helena d'Arenberg), her family and forebears provides us with a fascinating family mystery as well as illuminating the origins of the d'Arenberg label. The story begins with Helen's great-grandparents, Ignatius George and Louisa Jane Abeltshauser.

Ignatius George and Louisa Jane Abeltshauser

Frederick Augustus d'Arenberg, Helen Osborn's father, was born in Dublin on 29 September 1850. He was the second son and second child of the Reverend

Professor Ignatius George Abeltshauser and his second wife, Louisa Jane (née Thomas) Abeltshauser. Their other children were John George (b. c. 1849), Louisa Jane (b. 1853), Gustavus Adolphus (b. 1854), Arthur William (b. c. 1858) and Sophie Armstrong (b. 1861).

On 24 July 1869, at the age of 19, Frederick d'Arenberg entered Trinity College, Dublin.[53] He graduated BA in 1873 and MA in 1876.[54] He was admitted to the Inner Temple on 29 May 1874 and fulfilled all requirements but was never called to the Bar.[55] When he enrolled at Trinity, Frederick Augustus did so under the surname Abeltshauser, and this is where we begin to unravel the Abeltshauser and d'Arenberg mystery! A marginal note on Frederick's entrance admission reads 'changed to Arenburg [sic] per tutor's order November 21, 1871'.[56] This is noteworthy for two reasons: first, the name change was made five years after the death of his father, Ignatius George Abeltshauser; secondly, the alteration came exactly eight months after a notice was placed in *The Times* of London on 21 March 1871 by Louisa Jane Abeltshauser. The notice read:

THIS is to give notice that the WIDOW and CHILDREN of the late Rev. IGNATIUS GEORGE ABELTHAUSER [sic], L.L.D., Professor of French and German in the University of Dublin, intend henceforth to USE and be known by the NAME of D'ARENBERG.

LOUISA JANE D'ARENBERG (late Abeltshauser), 4 Cambridge Gardens, Notting Hill, March 20th, 1871.

117

The message having reached Trinity College, the requisite change (albeit misspelt) was made to Frederick's and his older brother John George's enrolment records. Both names were cross-referenced from Abeltshauser to 'Arenburg'.[57]

Why did Louisa Jane Abeltshauser decide to change her name and that of her children a full five years after her husband's death? Her husband, Ignatius George Abeltshauser, born in 1805, was the son of John George d'Arenberg and Rosina d'Arles. Stories of her father-in-law John George d'Arenberg's flight to Ireland in 1812, and the change of name to Abeltshauser, would of course have been known to Louisa Jane. Perhaps she had investigated the family background after her husband's death and decided to reclaim the Arenberg name. Can Sir David Kelly's later insinuation that John George d'Arenberg (born in either 1768 or 1771), who is referred to as being an offshoot, a Displaced Person and 'an outcast, from the reigning ducal house of Arenberg', be the key to this story? Suggestions that a child was born 'on the wrong side of the blanket' were made in the 1970s and tentatively put forward as a possible explanation for the change of name from the aristocratic d'Arenberg to a name (brushed off as fictitious) and later associated with musical talent, Abeltshauser. It is sad and frustrating that it is now not possible to discover the entire truth of this tantalising mystery. Nevertheless, having adopted a name belonging to an ancient European ducal house, the Abeltshauser-cum-Arenberg children began to make their way in the world.

John George and Frederick d'Arenberg

Ignatius George and Louisa Jane's oldest son, John George, born c. 1849, entered Trinity College, Dublin, on 26 June 1868; newspaper reports at the time of his death indicate that he obtained a double first in 1870. From 1871 until 1882 he paid his standard £10 admission fee after joining the Middle Temple as a student member. Apart from sitting examinations, a member was normally required to 'keep' 12 terms before he could be called to the Bar. It appears that John kept only 10 terms. This meant he was not called to the Bar and, therefore, could not practise as a barrister in Britain. Instead of a career in law, he chose, or more likely fell into, journalism. In 1876 he joined the literary staff of the *New York Herald* under Gordon Bennett, where he remained until he came to Australia in 1890. He then worked for the Adelaide *Advertiser* and the Melbourne *Age*.[58] He died at Frederick d'Arenberg's Adelaide home on 1 December 1898 and he was buried the following day at North Road Cemetery. A paragraph in the Adelaide *Advertiser* the following day reported that Mr F A d'Arenberg, his wife and her mother (Mrs Williams) were the chief mourners. He was buried in the d'Arenberg/Kelly grave along with his sister, Louisa Jane Kelly, her husband, David Kelly (died 21 March 1894), their son and two of their daughters, although the headstone does not reflect this.

At the age of 29, Frederick Augustus d'Arenberg migrated to Australia, arriving in Adelaide on the *Assam* on 27 February 1879. He travelled with his sister Louisa Jane and her husband, David Victor Frederick Kelly, the newly appointed Hughes Professor of Classics and Comparative Philology and Literature at the University of Adelaide. The Kellys settled in Adelaide and Frederick lived for some time with his sister and brother-in-law. Louisa died on 20 November 1886, only months after her brother-in-law Gustavus Abeltshauser-d'Arenberg. Professor Kelly then married Louisa's sister Sophie in 1889. Sophie had arrived in Adelaide on 19 November 1886 to help nurse her sister, who died only one day later. David and Sophie Kelly had two sons, but their marriage was short-lived, as Kelly died in 1894. Before leaving Australia, Sophie married Richard John Walker; they then returned to Ireland before moving to England.

Frederick and John's younger brother, Gustavus Adolphus, born 23 December 1854, adopted both names and called himself Abeltshauser-d'Arenberg.[59] He also migrated to Australia and worked as a bank clerk in Adelaide; he died on 13 July 1886 and was buried at North Road Cemetery, Adelaide. There were thus at least five members of the Abeltshauser family in South Australia at various times from 1879, all of whom used the name d'Arenberg.

Another view of the d'Arenberg story

Former British diplomat Sir David Kelly, one of the sons of Professor Kelly and his second wife, Sophie, tells this story of his family in his memoirs, *The Ruling Few*:

My mother, Sophie Armstrong d'Arenberg, was born in County Wicklow in Southern Island, though equally a member of the 'ascendancy'. Her grandfather, John George d'Arenberg, born at Mannheim in 1771, might be called a Displaced

Person, being an offshoot, and I fear an outcast, from the reigning ducal house of Arenberg which was mediatized with a hundred other German princes by Napoleon, i.e., they ceased to be independent royal princes and remained only great landowners. After service in Napoleon's armies, including the Moscow campaign of 1812, he went to Ireland (having killed in a duel a man more important than himself), taking with him his son, Ignatius George, born at Strasbourg in 1805, and adopted at the time of his flight the fictitious name of Abeltshauser. Under this rather absurd name his son went to Trinity College, Dublin. Having taken orders in the Church of Ireland, he was simultaneously Queen's Professor of French and German from 1842 to 1866, Prebendary of St Andrew's in St Patrick's Cathedral, and vicar of Derrylossary, County Wicklow — where my mother was born in Annamoe Rectory close to the famous Glendalough… In 1847 he married his second wife, Louisa Jane Thomas, daughter of Benjamin Thomas and niece of another Benjamin Thomas, an official of the old India Company whose work earned him a reference in a leading article in The Times… My mother related with some regret that as a girl in London she had declined an invitation there to see the future King Edward VII at a dance in a mood of Puritanical aversion to dancing… My mother told me that at the time of her father's death at Trinity College Dublin, on May 14th, 1866, he had been definitely promised the next vacant bishopric.[60]

Kelly reiterates that his grandfather's numerous children resumed the original name of d'Arenberg, and equally 'resumed the nomadic tradition of their grandfather (one of them, John George d'Arenberg joined the Carlists in Spain and subsequently became an editor in New York)'.[61] After his own father's death,

his mother returned for three years to Ireland, and then moved to London when he was six years old. He revealed that their migration to London was for the benefit of his half brother's and his own education.[62]

Kelly's description of the Abeltshauser–d'Arenberg connection accords with the story told by Helen to her husband, Frank. Her son Rowen's extensive research over decades has failed to locate either the birth or marriage certificate of John George d'Arenberg, the forebear who fled to Ireland after the fatal duel and adopted the name Abeltshauser. A family tree showing John George d'Arenberg as the son of Ignatius, Count d'Arenberg, and his marriage to Rosina d'Arles seems to exist, as does a marriage certificate. John George's birth certificate, 'in Latin on linen', was said to be with Fritz d'Arenberg in Australia but has not been found.

Fritz d'Arenberg arrives in Australia

After arriving in Adelaide, Helen d'Arenberg's father, Frederick Augustus, who became known as Fritz, provided 'Primary Instruction in French'. By 1881–82 he was examining candidates in French at both Junior and Matriculation levels on behalf of the university. For this he was paid £3 3s 0d for each paper set, with £1 1s 0d added for every 10 or fraction of 10 candidates after the first 10. Meanwhile he was serving articles with G A Farr, an Adelaide solicitor; by 1885 he was practising as a solicitor at Morialta Chambers, Victoria Square West. He continued to practise for the rest of his life, taking up rooms in Selbourne Chambers, Pirie Street. He lectured in Law at Adelaide University from 1897 to

1919; in 1907 he applied, unsuccessfully, for the Professorship of Law. He also worked as an academic coach but was probably best known for his work in the Adelaide Local Court. In the 1940s he was remembered by solicitor R H Cheek as one of the personalities who lent character to that jurisdiction. Press reports indicate that he had an active practice. Perhaps it was not surprising with all this work that he did not cope so well when he was one of three who were called upon to share the workload when Professor Salmond took a year's leave. The Chief Justice, Sir Samuel Way, commented that 'd'Arenberg, besides his own subjects, is doing Roman Law, and I fear making a very poor fist of it'.

In contrast to his apparently mediocre practice of law, in romance Fritz appears to have been successful. On 19 December 1894, at the age of 43, he married Eva Roubel Williams, 21 years his junior.[63] Eva was the eldest child of the Reverend Francis (1830–1895) and Celia Roubel Laurie Williams (1852–1922). Her father was born in Westminster, ordained deacon in 1852 and graduated BA in Mathematics in 1854 after studying at Lincoln College, Oxford. In 1860 he graduated MA and was offered the position of Third Master at St Peter's School Collegiate, Adelaide (now St Peter's College). After acting as Headmaster in 1881 he was appointed to the position in 1883, remaining there until 1889 when he resigned because of ill health.

Fritz d'Arenberg died on 3 October 1923 and was buried at North Road Cemetery, Adelaide; Reverend Dean Young officiated. He had lived all his married life at 44 Miller Street, North Unley. After the death of her husband and then her daughter, Eva Roubel d'Arenberg left Australia and spent the remainder of her life in China.

The Prince's challenge

Prince Erik, Duke d'Arenberg, writing from the Villa d'Arenberg, Lido, Punta del Este, Uruguay, on 23 June 1974, addressed his letter to the 'Head Management' of F E Osborn & Sons Pty Ltd in the following way:

Dear Sirs

I was accidentally shown a label and printed notice of the 'White d'Arenberg' you produce and sell. The label has furthermore the coat of arms of my family figuring on it.

As I am the head of the family d'Arenberg and having never heard of one of the family members growing wine in Australia and heard of one even living in Australia I would be greatly interested to hear, what is the origin of the giving of this name and these coat of arms to this White Burgundy you are producing.

I would be very thankfull [sic] for some information and am looking forward to your early answer.

Yours very sincerely
Duke d'Arenberg

The letter is straightforward and to the point. d'Arry, Toni and Rowen conferred then sought legal advice. They drafted several responses, which were not sent. Finally they replied to the Prince on 2 August 1974.

d'Arry thanked the Duke for his letter and explained to him that he was the

second son of F E Osborn, who had married Frances Helena d'Arenberg, a direct descendant of Ignatius, Count d'Arenberg, who married Rosina d'Arles in 1770. He mentioned that, for his part, he was unaware that any branch of the family lived in Uruguay, believing rather that the head of the family was Prince Arman d'Arenberg, who resided at the Chateau of Menetou Salon, near Bourges, in France.[64] d'Arry went on to explain that his mother had died in 1926 and that he had an older sister who lived in England and an older brother who served the Australian Government in the Department of Foreign Affairs, at that time in Canberra. No direct contact with the d'Arenberg side of the family had been maintained since his mother's death, he told the Prince. In a brief summary, d'Arry traced the history of his family's winery and explained that its wines were marketed in Australia, England, the USA and Canada. d'Arry disclosed that winemaking in the d'Arenberg name would be perpetuated in the next generation by his son Chester d'Arenberg Osborn, 'who at the age of 12 years is showing interest in carrying on our business'.[65] It was a confident letter sent in good faith. The Prince responded briefly on 18 August 1974, requesting further information about the Australian line of the family.

In a subsequent and lengthy letter from Prince Erik dated 20 January 1975, the Duke disputed any connection or right of Ignatius George Abeltshauser or Louisa Jane Abeltshauser to use the d'Arenberg name and, more particularly, the title or coat of arms. Indeed, he argued, official documents showed no link whatsoever between the d'Arenberg Ducal House and the Abeltshausers: 'Most regretfully must I conclude that this [name] belonging to the d'Arenberg family is but a legend.' He wrote:

*Given that your ancestors have no relationship links whatsoever with the
d'Arenberg House, they could not make use of our name for a 'trade and business'
purpose using it as wine brand (cf. Halsbury: The Laws of England, volume 29,
pages 356 and 357 no. 711 and vol. 21, pages 401 and 402)… In effect, the Arms
reproduced on the White d'Arenberg labels are the exact reproduction of the Arms
described in the Rietstap General Armorial that can be found in all large libraries
of the world. Finally the usurpation of our Arms for a commercial purpose is yet
reinforced by the motto 'Vinum Vita Est', printed on our coat of arms whilst the
motto of our House is 'Christus Protector Meus' and by existence of a commercial
society bearing the name of our House.*[66]

Finally, the Duke respectfully requested that the family cease using the name
'd'Arenberg' as a family name, cease using it on their wine and cease using the
d'Arenberg coat of arms. He added here that he would 'rather continue within
the terms of our courteous relations' and politely begged them to 'take the
measure spontaneously' rather than compelling him to resort to an 'injunction' to
discontinue 'this unquestionable prejudice that results from the use of our Arms
and our Name on a commercial label'.[67]

The Osborn family sought further legal advice. While their lawyers,
Mouldens, did not see any problem with the wine being marketed as d'Arenberg in
Australia, the use of the coat of arms presented difficult legal questions. The name
d'Arenberg was registered as a trademark under the *Trade Marks Act 1955–1966*.
However, if the Duke or any other family members carried on a wine business
in the UK under the name d'Arenberg, Mouldens were sure the Osborns would

encounter difficulties. As to continued use of the coat of arms, Mouldens advised the following:

> *Use of the name d'Arenberg in conjunction with the coat of arms of the house of d'Arenberg on a wine label would seem to go a little further than mere decoration or embellishment since it seems to be alleging some kind of direct connection with the house of d'Arenberg. We believe that as a matter of common sense if the High Court of Chivalry were to sit on such a case it would be very reluctant indeed to interfere, particularly since the dignity involved would be a foreign dignity.*[68]

In sum, Mouldens advised d'Arry, Toni and Rowen to change the d'Arenberg coat of arms created by d'Arry and Don Allnut in 1959. Two letters in the files appear to provide the story. We know that a letter dated 20 June 1975 was sent to the Duke d'Arenberg. A draft letter in the files addresses the points raised in the Duke's January letter, although it is not clear that this is a copy of the letter that was finally sent. The draft states that nothing in Australian law prevents the use of the name 'd'Arenberg' by the Australian family or by their companies, as long as they are not guilty of passing off their goods as the goods of others. The letter assured the Duke that the Osborn family and their businesses were not guilty of that, either in Australia or elsewhere. It was also the writer's opinion that the pages the Duke quoted from Halsbury's *Laws of England* supporting his case in fact did the opposite. He concluded: 'Out of deference to you but not with any admission of wrongful conduct I propose to change the coat of arms'.[69] When this draft letter is read in conjunction with the Duke's response dated 27 July, it

is almost certain the two letters form the chronological chain of correspondence. The Duke conceded that the use of the name d'Arenberg was done in good faith. He held on to his belief that at some time in the past, a 'side-step happened in the Arenberg family with the result of some natural child' and that the natural child could not be accepted into the family, nor could it be accorded titles or use of the coat of arms. While Duke d'Arenberg retained this contention, there is no evidence to prove it one way or another.

Had d'Arry even considered that this might happen when he enthusiastically adopted the d'Arenberg coat of arms on his label in 1959? The answer is, clearly, he had not. When asked about it recently he explained it like this:

> Prince Erik d'Arenberg … wrote to me and said, 'I didn't think I had any relatives in Australia, how come you use my royal family crest on your bottle?' He was the owner of the crest and he happened to be the head of the … ducal family of Arenberg at that time. I used his crest but I had no right to it … He had a point and I felt quite embarrassed that we'd pinched his crest … I didn't even know they existed, I hadn't thought about it, it didn't occur to me. I was very naive about that. It was 1959 [when] we did the label, and this was 1972 or somewhere before it was found out. As a result, we changed the crest into what it is today, which is a made-up crest that's got an Egyptian ankh on it (which we were using in the Bushing Festival), which is a symbol of eternal life, I think.[70]

Some years after he received the June 1974 letter from the Duke d'Arenberg, d'Arry received yet another letter along similar lines, this time signed by Prince Leopold d'Arenberg of Lausanne. The letter is dated 9 January but a year is not included; Rowen believes it was either 1978 or 1979. Prince Leopold's letter stated that he had recently visited Australia and noticed d'Arenberg wines on sale; indeed that he was very pleased to see that d'Arenberg wine could be bought in Australia! (At the time, the relationship between Prince Leopold and Prince Erik d'Arenberg was unclear.) As it happened, Prince Leopold was himself a winemaker and the essence of the letter was to propose a partnership in the wine business. The Prince suggested that 'Instead of using the d'Arenberg name for your wine, you should use the label Prince d'Arenberg either for a specific type of your wine — the best one — or for the whole lot'. He also proposed that he 'could even take a minority share (below 5%) in your company or in a new company whose objective should be the sale of Prince d'Arenberg wine'.[71] This proposal was negotiated as recently as 2006.[72] The files are now full of correspondence between the Osborn family and various members of the d'Arenberg families.

Rowen Osborn worked as an Australian diplomat for 40 years and spent many of those years posted overseas. Prompted by the Duke d'Arenberg's challenges in 1974 and 1975, Rowen became an enthusiastic family historian during his overseas postings. He traced the Abeltshauser and d'Arenberg family histories, spoke to and exchanged correspondence for many years with descendants of the children of Professor Kelly and Sophie (née Armstrong d'Arenberg), and thoroughly documented the early history of both the d'Arenberg and Osborn families in Australia. Rowen is well informed of this history, although he has never been able to make a direct family link dating back further than Count Ignatius d'Arenberg. Rowen's detective work also traced both Prince Leopold and Prince Erik and their families. He discovered that Prince and Princess Armand d'Arenberg were selling white wine made on their estate, the Chateau of Mentou-Salon, southwest of Paris. He also found that Prince Armand was dismissed by Prince Erik as of a minor branch of the family; he was a third cousin once removed. The d'Arenberg dynasty continues in Europe with occasional murmurings to and from the unofficial Australian arm of the family.

Celebrating Osborn milestones

Meantime the various Osborn family members were growing up. Rowen and Beverley continued to travel the world. Their daughter, Eliza, born in 1967, travelled with them and became fluent in several languages while attending international schools. Toni and Pat Bourne still lived in Kent, with their two sons, Christopher and Timothy. Toni and Rowen, both shareholders in the family business, remained actively interested in the progress of the vineyard. Winemaking was an entrenched Osborn family occupation.

In 1978 the Osborn family celebrated the 50th anniversary of winemaking by F E Osborn & Sons; and d'Arry was awarded the Queen's Jubilee Medal for his services to the Australian wine industry. The 50th anniversary was marked by a full year of jubilee dinners and celebrations held around the country. Australian and international wine critics and writers, wine distributors, hoteliers and lovers of d'Arenberg wines were entertained in Melbourne, Sydney, Brisbane and Perth — a 'who's who' of the wine world participated in the festivities. Wine tastings, dinners and lectures and many other events took place throughout the year. In 1983 d'Arry himself celebrated 50 years of winemaking and was suitably honoured. In 2004 he was awarded the Queen's Medal of the Order of Australia (OAM) for his contribution to the wine industry and the McLaren Vale region over half a century.

In 50 years the family winemaking enterprise had grown beyond anything Frank could have imagined when he arrived in McLaren Vale before the Great War. Guided to some extent by his father Joseph, Frank was respected for his pioneering efforts in the industry. At a pivotal moment in Australian winemaking history he embraced the opportunity to become a winemaker rather than merely a supplier of grapes. Reflecting on the period up to 1957, d'Arry recalls that his father's skill was not in doing the physical work himself, but in managing others around him. His was an example of a modest grape growing and winemaking business that maintained a sturdily independent existence, and he was acknowledged for this.[73] Encumbered by chronic ill health, Frank was fortunate that his bright and intelligent son d'Arry, who had always wanted to be a winemaker — as, in turn, did his own son, Chester — proved to be more than capable of carrying on the work.

From the heady days of establishing a new and individual wine label that reflected and honoured the d'Arenberg family name to the tumultuous 1960s, when years of shortage and glut tested winemakers throughout Australia, to the great expansion of the 1970s, F E Osborn & Sons and d'Arenberg Wines consciously positioned themselves as a major contributor to the Australian wine industry. They won the prized Jimmy Watson Memorial Trophy for their one-year-old red, contended with challenges to their name and label, established profitable independent distribution networks, exported overseas ahead of the crowd, and continued to win prizes in wine shows. d'Arry had prepared the ground for Chester eventually to take over as winemaker, an idea they had both long cherished, but was the family or the winemaking world of the early 1980s ready for Chester's individualism, his ability to think laterally and long term, and his innate talent for pushing the boundaries?

CHAPTER 6

Chester d'Arenberg Osborn — 'a child of the vinous universe'

Being able to make wine is a joy. I say to people I've never worked a day in my life, and Dad always says he can vouch for that![1]

CHESTER'S CAREER WAS PREDETERMINED. LIKE HIS FATHER, HE HAD ALWAYS known what he wanted to do. At the age of two he was told by his mother that he would be an inventive winemaker. How did she know? His father, too, knew that winemaking was in his son's blood, as it had been in his. Chester worked in the vineyard and winery during school holidays from an early age, and clearly wanted to follow in his father's footsteps. d'Arry paid him 10 cents an hour for picking grapes, pumping wine, filling bottles and sticking labels on them. d'Arry had also made it clear in correspondence with the European d'Arenbergs in the 1970s that Chester would become the next winemaker. At the age of seven, when he sat on Len Evans's knee one night as the grown-ups were discussing business, Chester declared that he wanted to be a winemaker and when Evans asked, 'What sort of wine are you going to make?' Chester replied, 'A yummy one'.[2] There were strong early signs, then, that he was, as

Australian Gourmet Traveller magazine would later put it, 'a child of the vinous universe'.[3]

Making yummy wine

Chester clearly had the desire to make wine, and it was not long before his flair for the arts and other creative pursuits was also apparent. As a child he started making plastic model airplanes and then moved on to balsawood planes that would fly. Growing up on a farm, he made a car out of two-inch water pipe and an engine from an old Ford Prefect (and so learned about mechanics from a young age). While at school he studied photography and in 1979 won an Australia-wide school competition for the best black and white photograph. He has delved into oil painting, computer-generated painting, sculpture, architecture and creative writing.[4] Chester's house is filled with his own oil paintings and sculptures. However, winemaking is his first love. Since 1984 he has carved out his own niche in the wine industry. Some journalists focus on his loud shirts and distinctive shaggy hairstyle; they are not the real story, they are simply emblematic of the man.

In 2009 Chester made quite an impression on English wine journalist Andrew Jefford, who wrote:

> *First, there's the hair. Any man in his mid-40s with cascading, long blond ringlets is playing a fairly adventurous hand against time. Happily, Chester's aren't fussily tended and look as if they just happened, like tonsorial bougainvillea. Then there's*

the multicoloured shirts and floral jeans — very Haight-Ashbury. He's a biggish, sloppy-looking guy with a shambling gait, blue eyes and a tenacious grin — and he never stops talking.[5]

It is, however, his obvious skill and passion for winemaking, working with the McLaren Vale *terroir* and pushing the boundaries by experimenting with different grape varieties, that have earned him the title of 'one of the most creative, imaginative and charismatic winemakers in Australia'.[6] According to the same writer, Australian journalist Andrew Caillard, his 'diversity of interest, personal conviction and leadership' make him one of Australia's great winemakers.[7]

As has been observed, it is hard for any son of a legend 'to live in his old man's shadow'.[8] Notwithstanding the similarities and differences in their education and upbringing, more than anything both father and son wanted to make wine — and so they did. d'Arry learned to make wine as he worked in the vineyard from the age of 16; his father knew the importance of learning 'on the job'. But Chester also studied formally and qualified as winemaker and viticulturalist. After attending McLaren Vale Primary School and Prince Alfred College, he entered Roseworthy Agricultural College in 1980. As an undergraduate, Chester worked vintages at other wineries, including Tullochs in the Hunter Valley and Hardy's Chateau Reynella. He graduated from Roseworthy with a Bachelor of Applied Science, Oenology, in 1983. Knowing his affinity with painting, it is unsurprising that Chester has since described Roseworthy College as like 'attending school without touching a canvas or paintbrush'. But he was a motivated student and he wrote his thesis on tannin management 'about 10 years before it became a popular issue'.[9]

After his graduation and after the 1984 vintage, d'Arry allowed Chester to spend six months touring the vineyards and wineries of France, Italy, Germany and Spain. According to d'Arry, he 'sent him off around the world with Joe Grilli and Eddie Smith'.[10] While in Europe he tasted, watched and listened, absorbing as much as he could of what the winemakers were doing.[11] His 'frenetic' travels around Europe sparked a love of flowery wines with mineral elegance that has evolved into a lifelong pursuit.[12]

On his return to McLaren Vale, in 1984 Chester took over as d'Arenberg's chief winemaker. d'Arry allowed Chester to have the 'run of the winery' without parental interference:

> *He had already worked with us and knew the ropes. He did things he wanted to do, including making white wine. I had left it five years too late to modernise the winery, which needed more refrigeration and crushers and things, and Chester rapidly did all that although he kept the old basket presses, which we still use.*[13]

d'Arry is very proud of his son and always exhibited the greatest confidence in his ability. Following on from his Roseworthy thesis, tannin management has been a central theme of d'Arenberg winemaking since 1984. Chester today affirms that he is particularly interested in tannin quality because it is profoundly linked to the flavour profile and the nuances of individual vineyard style. He describes these in different ways: muscular, chalky, crunchy, ironlike, sooty and earthy. Andrew Jefford loves hearing Chester talk about wines 'because the words betray the way he is moving around an intimate world with great familiarity, finding "gritty tannins" here and a "sooty iron character" there, before setting off in pursuit of "turgidity" or "boniness".[14] Chester believes that it is these elements, blended and layered, that bring a seamless and evocative soil character to d'Arenberg's wines.[15]

Chester's first vintage

Nineteen eighty-four was an auspicious year for many reasons. It was the year d'Arry celebrated the 25th anniversary of the famous d'Arenberg red stripe label. It was also Chester's first vintage, which included the first d'Arenberg barrel-fermented Chardonnay. This was an immediate success; sales in white wines increased dramatically Australia-wide when d'Arenberg were making one-third white wine and two-thirds red. And 1984 was the year d'Arenberg white wines were launched in the first-class cabins of Qantas Airlines' international flights. The following year Chester's 1985 White Burgundy was awarded a trophy at the McLaren Vale Wine Show. It was the first vintage of the 'Noble Riesling' and the 'Old Vine Shiraz' — to their knowledge, these were the first wines in the world to be labelled as 'Noble' and 'Old Vine'. The first vintage of the 'Ironstone Pressings' was produced in 1987. Some of McLaren Vale's vineyards are impregnated with ancient, decomposed laterite granite known as ironstone and its extraordinary rusty red-brown colour is derived from the iron oxides present in the stone.[16] The description of the soil that produced the wine dates back to the 1890s when it appears Thomas Hardy, in describing the wines of the McLaren Vale, coined the term 'ferruginous'. This term was taken up by exporter/importer P B Burgoyne when referring to the iron content and consequent health-giving qualities of the Australian wine. Today 'Ironstone Pressings' is a combination of Grenache (70 per cent), Shiraz (25 per cent) and Mouvèdre (5 per cent), making it a quintessential McLaren Vale wine.

Before the 1988 vintage more than $100 000 was spent on the winery. A rotary drum vacuum filter was installed along with heat exchangers, which are used for white grapes as soon as they are crushed. The grapes go straight through the heat exchanger to reduce their temperature to between 1 and 10°C. Chester introduced clean juice technology and inert gas to a greater extent than his father. As a result, the wines became fresher, cleaner and crisper, and stayed more youthful longer.

Chester's first vintage in 1984 marked significant changes in the equipment and techniques employed at d'Arenberg. In 1988 *Winestate* magazine published a profile of the father-and-son team, highlighting the changes occurring at the vineyard and winery. The magazine used the succession story as a metaphor for the changes occurring in Australian winemaking and 'how the torch is passing from the old school to the new'.[17] By focusing on the fact that in the past d'Arry would have decided on the right time to pick grapes by looking at the sky to see what the weather promised and by tasting the grapes to see if they were ready, trusting his judgement and years of experience, the article implied that Chester relied on modern technology to decide the right time to pick. However, Chester assures us that the traditional approach is still used today, with the added analysis of sugar levels. d'Arry's methods were contrasted with the 'new thumbprint' and supposed 'subtle changes' being instigated by Chester. He was indeed making changes, and they were not in the least subtle. Labelled 'the new kid on the block',

RIGHT *Chester and d'Arry tasting wine from the oak barrel, c. 1980.*

ABOVE *Loading d'Arenberg's first container bound for Holland in 1988; d'Arry standing in doorway.*

d'Arry standing in winery upstairs doorway with Chester on the tractor, c. 1990.

ABOVE *Chester, Rowen, Jackie and d'Arry Osborn host a wine dinner, c. 1990.*

ABOVE *The one that didn't get away! d'Arry Osborn proudly displaying his catch of a massive snapper at Coffin Bay, June 2009.*

LEFT *The Osborns of McLaren Vale in 2004: d'Arry (78), Toni (83) and Rowen (80).*

LEFT *d'Arry and Chester at the cellar door with some of their portfolio.*

RIGHT *Chester and d'Arry at work at the basket press, 2009.*

Chester dressed as a 'derelict vineyard' at a d'Arenberg growers' dinner.

Aerial photograph of d'Arenberg winery and vineyard, summer 2009.

ABOVE *d'Arenberg cellar door and old dairy.*

BELOW *Chester with his three daughters, Alicia, Mia and Ruby in 2011.*

ABOVE *Chester and his partner, Kathie Tidemann.*

Open fermenters currently in use at d'Arenberg.

in the late 1980s Chester began 'playing around' with the red wines by adding more pressings back because he had been using cold fermentation, which is less extractive. He was also introducing more and more new oak, trialling different parcels of wine in oak and seeing how they differed in time. He argued that using less of the pressings and relying more on the tannin from new oak would give the backbone, the flavour and the lift to the wine.[18]

One question that arose for Chester in his early days as winemaker was: to fine or not to fine the wine? He has done little of it since taking over in 1984. A new winemaking philosophy has developed since he became winemaker and traditional practices used from the 1950s through until the 1980s have slowly been revised. The use of small, headed-down open fermenters, for example, a traditional practice with ancient origins, was incorporated; and 'almost every other technique has been modified or changed to reduce the mechanical breakdown of fruit and over-extraction of phenolics'.[19]

WBM: Australia's Wine Business Magazine's 2009 'Regional Heroes' story assesses, among other things, the similarities and differences between Chester's winemaking and that of his father. It also reveals the deep love and affection they have for each other. Chester believes their winemaking styles are not fundamentally different:

> *Dad was caught up in World War Two and there was no money to employ anyone or buy anything. He was doing it all hands-on and didn't have the time to analyse things or do things differently. We're still making wine exactly the same way he did — same vineyards; no fertilisers; no cultivation...we're still using the open*

fermenters that were built in 1927; we still use foot treading and most reds are not racked, with no filtering or fining. We still basket press every grape, even for the Stump Jump range. We have gentler crushers now, though, and more refrigeration, but we still get the wines quite warm in the ferment. And of course we use smaller barrels than the big woods Dad used.[20]

Yet the story is not quite as straightforward as he makes it sound. As we shall see, significant changes were instigated in 1984 while others were introduced gradually as Chester honed his skills. As he recently put it, you can't learn how to make wine until you do it yourself in your own place.[21]

Another turbulent decade in Australian winemaking

The decade between 1985 and 1994 was as turbulent for the Australian wine industry as any it had experienced.[22] As James Halliday writes, a harbinger of what lay ahead for the Australian industry was the 10 per cent wholesale sales tax on wine introduced in August 1984 following the mini-recession of 1982–83. The tax was absorbed by winemakers and not passed on to the consumer. The government increased the sales tax on wine to 20 per cent in 1986, despite the fact that any increase in the price of wine over the period 1984–85 to 1985–86 was kept below the rise in the Consumer Price Index. Wine consumption increased while beer consumption decreased, so by 1984–85 wine was cheaper than beer, lemonade or Coca-Cola.[23] White wine was still the most popular table wine, and Chardonnay was the drink of the day, experiencing a major boom from the mid 1980s onwards.

The most important development of the decade was the growth in exports of Australian wine. Ironically, the great interest in exporting wine was due to the overplanting in the 1970s and the subsequent surplus of wine produced in the 1980s. It was only once the export boom began that some Australian producers started to develop the potential of the largely unexploited international market. In 1984–85 wine imports reached an all-time high. Almost 30 years on, Australian wine exports are even higher than the 1984–85 levels. The weak French franc and the strong Australian dollar, floated by the Labor government in December 1983, encouraged a surge in imported wine, especially French. Australia imported 13.1 million litres of wine, substantially more than the 8.3 million litres of wine exported.[24]

As Chardonnay began its ascendancy in the 1980s Rhine Riesling began to lose favour with the wine-drinking public. By the late 1980s the strong preference for white wine was beginning to wane, with red wines, especially Cabernet Sauvignon, gaining in popularity. Growers who were able to adapt to the new trend began grubbing out their white and fortified varities, such as Rhine Riesling, Shiraz and Grenache, and grafting Chardonnay onto existing vines. In 1986 the South Australian government instigated a 'vine pull' scheme to get rid of the now out-of-style varieties, resulting in the destruction of many old Shiraz, Grenache, Doradillo, Palomino and other vines that are today experiencing a renaissance. The d'Arenberg Burgundy, a wine made by d'Arry blending 50 per cent Shiraz and Grenache, less popular grape varieties, was not immune from criticism, as we shall see.

As the 1980s progressed, the major companies — Penfolds, Lindeman's, Orlando — produced and sold a large proportion of generically labelled casks, filled with Sultana, muscat and gordo blanco varieties.[25] The general trends in wine sales in the 1980s was also changing: between 1982 and 1989 premium wine sales grew by 42 per cent while non-premium wine sales declined by 15 per cent. Low-priced 750 ml bottles formed the core business of the major chains, a practice that continues today. This trend did not deter d'Arry Osborn, who was responding well to the increasing demand for dry red table wines.

In his 1985 book *The Australian Wine Compendium*, James Halliday praised d'Arry's successes while affirming what most wine writers were writing: that attitudes to the existing Australian wine styles was changing. This theme was taken up by wine writers and critics throughout the 1980s and was used both to praise and to condemn winemakers. The d'Arenberg wine styles were described as 'unashamedly traditional' and exhibiting the McLaren Vale district's 'cowshed' character (caused by hydrogen sulphide created in the fermentation process). In this respect, Halliday felt the wines would be accepted only by the 'older generation of wine drinkers'. The young generation, he believed, were rejecting this flavour. Halliday further argued that 'the style of d'Arenberg wines will slowly evolve into a more conventional pattern' because 'd'Arry's son Chester, a Roseworthy graduate, now shares the winemaking responsibilities with his father'.[26] This prediction proved to be accurate.

d'Arry himself knew that his winemaking had to change to keep up with fashion trends so was eager for Chester to experiment and implement the changes he felt were needed. In 1986 wine writer Robin Bradley described the d'Arenberg Burgundy as 'a product of d'Arry's individualism and independent attitude towards winemaking'. While others were 'blushingly guilty' about their Grenache plantings, Bradley suggested, in blending his Grenache with Shiraz and Shiraz pressings, which gave the wine old wood and bottle age, d'Arry was swimming against the tide of fashion, continuing to blend two unfashionable grapes. This did not worry d'Arry. Bradley himself admitted that the blend created one of the area's most attractive wines.[27] Bradley failed to recognise Chester's winemaking skills in this book, but by the early 1990s Chester's name was everywhere. Probably not to his surprise, but certainly to his gratification, his efforts were soon acknowledged by many wine industry awards in recognition of his talent and passion. At the McLaren Vale Bushing Festival in 1990 Chester was named 'Bushing King' for his 1987 Noble Riesling.

In 1989 the Federation of Australian Winemaker Associations brought together the Australian Wine and Brandy Producers' Association, the Australian Winemakers' Forum and the Wine and Brandy Co-operative Producers' Association of Australia. In 1990 the name was changed to the Winemakers' Federation of Australia, but its rationale stayed the same. The three antecedent organisations recognised that there was greater gain in a single and united voice. Each formed an Electoral College and nominated representatives to the federation to make decisions on strategic issues and policy on behalf of the entire industry. Soon a new structure evolved, and state associations now play a vital role. In 2006 members voted to change the federation's organisational structure by creating three membership categories. d'Arenberg has a membership in the medium category, for winemakers producing between 2000 and 100 000 tonnes per annum.

Changing tastes and new styles

James Halliday, an ongoing champion of d'Arry Osborn and d'Arenberg wines, added the 1988 d'Arenberg Burgundy to his 1992 list of Australia's *100 Best Wines*, proof that both the public and the wine critics' taste in wine could be fickle. 'A blend of Shiraz and Grenache picked from very old vines', Halliday wrote, 'it is crammed with spicy fruit yet is relatively soft and round in the mouth as befits a burgundy-style wine.' It was priced at $8.10 and was recommended as 'tailor-made for game'.[28] Only a year later, in a review of the 1989 d'Arenberg Burgundy, wine writer Ralph Kyte-Powell gave the 'traditional' McLaren Vale style a mixed report, pointing to the fact that the wine was 'sometimes port-like' and had a distinctive 'barn-yard' smell. In saying this, he acknowledged that 1993 marked d'Arry's 50th vintage and that the features of the wine reflected d'Arry's traditional approach. However, he did observe that Chester had injected a modern influence and he enthused about d'Arenberg's use of Grenache:

> *Much of the wine's character has been due to the use of Grenache grapes from very old vines, along with the more common Shiraz. Grenache, the staple of many French wines, both good and bad, was once widely used in Australia for red wines but fell out of fashion during the wine boom of the 1960s and 1970s.*

Kyte-Powell described the earthy nose and typical raspberry scent of the Grenache, with its medium-bodied rich flavour that remains dry and firmly tannic. He judged it to be a good wine for the traditionalists and one he thought would age well. He considered it would complement pasta and Italian-inspired dishes well and offered reasonable value at around $9.00.[29]

The 'barn-yard' or 'cowshed' smell of the d'Arenberg wines was often raised by wine writers to draw attention to generational differences — d'Arry's traditional winemaking versus Chester's innovations juxtaposed against changing popular food tastes — for example, the lighter, minimalist food style and presentation of nouvelle cuisine. In short, people's palates were changing and Chester was the face of new ideas and new methods.[30] The magazine *Winewise* emphasised this in its critical review of d'Arenberg Wines in 1994:

> *If there was an award for the most improved winery in Australia, d'Arenberg would have to be our choice. The transformation in both their red and white wines, commencing with the 1990 vintage, has been quite astonishing. Gone are the earthy, leathery odours so typical of McLaren Vale reds of the '60s and '70s, replaced by fresh, varietal flavours. The whites reflect state-of-the-art winemaking, from complex barrel-fermented chardonnays, to crisp acid-fresh rhine rieslings (easily the best in McLaren Vale), to botrytised sweet whites which now challenge those of De Bortoli as Australia's best... Chester showed us the last three vintages of rhine riesling, chardonnay, Old Vines Shiraz, and d'Arry's Original Burgundy, as well as his '91 and '92 sweet whites, clearly demonstrating the giant strides he has made with the wines of the '90s.*[31]

The turnaround at d'Arenberg Wines of the 1990s, the authors argued, meant the vineyard could now be considered to be among not only McLaren Vale's but Australia's best premium wine producers. Halliday and Evans already considered them among Australia's best. The work Chester was doing in the late 1980s resulted in many prestigious awards in the mid 1990s. While it was acknowledged that d'Arry exemplified the old school of Australian wine, it was also recognised that the winery itself had responded positively to the emergent new styles and changing tastes.[32]

In 1992 Chester's 'Ironstone Pressings' came to the notice of James Halliday, who described it as the 'big brother' of the d'Arenberg Burgundy.[33]

[The] 1989 d'Arenberg Ironstone Pressings is a wine made from the pressings of Shiraz and Grenache, so it has the same varietal composition [as the d'Arenberg Burgundy]...but is — as one might expect — bigger and fuller in weight than the Burgundy. On the other hand, it is not massively tannic or extractive: Chester Osborn has done a very clever balancing act to produce a velvety, full-flavoured wine with some of the same spicy characters evident, but even fuller fruit.[34]

Praise indeed from one of Australia's most knowledgeable and distinguished wine writers. Also in 1992 Chester Osborn came to the notice of many Australian women as a bachelor with 'star rating' when he was featured in *Cleo* magazine as one of Australia's 50 most sought-after men. This took Chester, then 29, by surprise! Interviewed by *Cleo* for the story, Chester later claimed that his comments had been misinterpreted. Nevertheless, on the strength of the article, he did receive a great deal of public attention.[35] For the local newspaper he revealed that, while he was still single, he was hoping to find a woman who, above all, would like d'Arenberg wines! In 1996 Chester married Bernadette Wieland.

Terroir and naming regulations

From the first days of winemaking in Australia, wines had been labelled according to their French, Italian, German or Spanish name. It was not until the mid twentieth century that small winemakers such as Eric Purbrick at Chateau Tahbilk, in the Goulburn Valley–Nagambie region of Victoria, began to bottle their wine under varietal names. The laws appear to have been lax on this issue until the 1990s, when the French exerted their influence over Australian wine labelling. Up until that time the regulations concerning grape variety, region of origin and vintage required only that if the name of any wine included an allusion to grape variety, locality or year of vintage, then the wine must contain 80 per cent of that variety, be at least 80 per cent from that region and contain 95 per cent of the year of vintage. In 1993 Australia signed a wine trade deal with the European Community, allowing better access to their market in return for 'tidying up the then-haphazard' approach to the naming of wine regions.[36]

The industry restructure and regulations for naming wines and wine regions occurred almost concurrently in Australia in the early 1990s. As the Australian wine writer Max Allen notes, 'Australia could boast many established and emerging wine districts, but their names and boundaries weren't protected by law, as European wine regions are'.[37] The Australian wine industry undertook a study that defined and described its viticultural landscapes, officially registered as Geographical Indications (GI) in the Register of Protected Names. Over about 10 years winemakers met and discussed, debated and decided on these boundaries so that there are now 100 such wine GIs. Incredibly, the very large GI 'South Eastern Australia' takes in South Australia, Victoria and New South Wales, and this label is often used on generic, non-specific bulk wine bottled as cleanskins or sold by the largest producers, such as Constellation and BRL Hardy.

McLaren Vale is part of the Fleurieu Peninsula Geographical Indication, although it is actually a subsection of the overall area. The specific *terroir* of d'Arenberg's vineyards is something Chester Osborn feels passionately about; it is, he believes, fundamental to his production of distinctive wines. d'Arenberg is located within the McLaren Vale subregion of Beautiful View (originally known as Bellevue) located just north of the township of McLaren Vale. The soils in this region are highly variable, from red earth clay on limestone to sand on marly limestone to grey loam on clay. The shallow soils are among the poorest in the region, resulting frequently in low yields and low vigour. Hilltops in the Beautiful View subregion experience warm nights and cool afternoon sea breezes, while valleys experience cold air drainage off the range as it flows towards the sea at night.

Following the impetus to define regional indications in 1989, the Australian Wine and Brandy Corporation (AWBC) was authorised to assist in the keeping of standard winery records. A new standard system of record keeping meant that weighbridge records had to show vintage, location of vineyard, grape variety, tonnage and name of grower. In the winery itself, the same records were required.

Through the use of the new 'universal recording system', it was possible for the auditor to validate the legitimacy of all vintage, variety and region of origin claims by the winemaker. Named the Label Integrity Program (LIP), its aim was to protect consumers of Australian wine, both at home and overseas.[38] This program was instigated at about the time the French began disallowing the use of the name 'Burgundy' by any winemaker outside France. d'Arenberg were then still selling wines with traditional European names such as White Burgundy, Red Burgundy, Claret and Rhine Riesling, although it did specify that it originated in the McLaren Vale. From the late 1980s, however, a sea change was occurring at d'Arenberg, and wines were being labelled more imaginatively. For example, the 1989 'White Ochre' was a classic dry white, the 1989 'Red Ochre' was a Shiraz/ Cabernet Sauvignon combination, and the 'High Trellis' was named because the block it was grown on was flooded early in the twentieth century and higher trellises were erected to handle the vines.

In 1993, after 50 years of labelling the wine 'Burgundy', d'Arenberg Wines renamed their '1989 d'Arenberg Burgundy' as 'd'Arry's Original Shiraz Grenache'.[39] The new label coincided with celebrations of d'Arry's Golden Jubilee in winemaking. To mark the occasion, dinners were held in Australian capital cities during April and May 1993. The gold-embossed invitation to the upmarket dinner held at Florentino Restaurant in Melbourne set the tone for the grand celebration:

> d'Arry Osborn's first vintage at McLaren Vale was in 1943. Half a century later d'Arry and his son Chester are completing the 1993 vintage at the same family winery.[40]

Halliday's words, published years before, summed up his achievement: 'few men or women have been around the Australian wine industry as long as d'Arry or have worked as tirelessly or selflessly for the industry'.[41] No doubt he was flattered, but d'Arry took such tributes in his stride. He could point to a record 20 trophies and 121 gold medals — a total of 700 medals. From 1992 the Winemakers' Federation of Australia began honouring individuals who have made a particularly significant contribution to the Australian wine and brandy industry by electing them to the College of Patrons or awarding them Life Membership of the Australian Wine Industry. In 1994 d'Arry was invested as a Patron for his outstanding contribution to the affairs of the industry.

After 10 years as chief winemaker, while d'Arry went fishing as often as possible, Chester was rapidly expand their portfolio of wines. In 1993 he began to choose grapes from the best barrels of the best vineyards to make new wines. As he turned more and more to high-quality wine, he introduced 'single individual concept wines' into the market. In 1994 he produced the 'Dead Arm Shiraz',[42] named after a fungal disease that killed off one arm of the vine, resulting in truncated, gap-toothed vines. The dead arm vines date back to the 1912 planting. The grapes are crushed in headed-down open fermenters, as well as basket presses, a longstanding practice dating back many centuries. Vinification techniques optimise richness of flavour and preserve aromas, purity of fruit and integrity of tannins. The wine completes fermentation and is then matured in a combination of new and seasoned American and French oak for around 20–22 months. The range of Chester's single individual concept wines continues to grow. New varieties and blends have enabled d'Arenberg to introduce a mid to upper price range for their wines. These are 'Chester's Champions'.[43]

In 1995 Chester oversaw the first plantings of white Rhône varieties, which included 10 acres of Marsanne, 9 acres of Roussanne and 14 acres of Viognier. This was also the year of the first vintage of the 'Coppermine Road Cabernet Sauvignon'. The barrel-fermented Chardonnay was renamed the 'Olive Grove Chardonnay' as oak was starting to become *de rigeur*. Each of the new labels of old wine varieties has a story. The first crop of Roussanne from the 2000 vintage was covered in a sea of tiny money spiders (Erigoninae). Popular belief is that kindness to these little creatures will bring good luck, especially in the form of money. Being a nature-lover and slightly superstitious, Chester refrained from sending the spiders to their death. Hence the first release of Roussanne was from the 2001 vintage, by which time the money spiders had learned their lesson and moved from the vineyard to surrounding bushland. According to Chester, 'Up until when the wine is in the bottle we are deadly serious about our winemaking — from then on it should all be about fun'.[44]

While d'Arenberg is generally known for its big, intense reds, such as the Dead Arm and the Ironstone Pressings, for Andrew Jefford it is the white wines that illustrate what an astute wine-blender Chester is. The Hermit Crab Viognier-Marsanne, which mingles fruit from the warm McLaren Vale region with 'a freshening contribution from high up in the Adelaide Hills', convinces Jefford of his expertise. He has written that many Australian winemakers are now making white wines from Rhône varieties but few can 'endow them with the perfume, flavour, detail and poise' that Chester has managed. Although slightly bemused at first by Chester's unconventional character, Jefford's view remains that the

best wine creators are 'slightly crazy' and 'inhabit a parallel universe to the rest of us'. Some might argue that this is indeed an accurate description of Chester d'Arenberg Osborn.

d'Arry's Verandah

Australian wineries were tourist attractions from as early as the 1960s, so offering a restaurant to attract visitors was not a new idea. d'Arry had worked tirelessly with other McLaren Vale winemakers from the late 1950s, as one of the original Bushing Festival presidents in the 1970s and as a promoter of tourism to the region. It was therefore no surprise that d'Arry, with his brother Rowen and sister Toni, the two other shareholders in the business, eventually took the plunge to open a restaurant. Like all innovations, this was a major financial investment for the company and the decision was not made lightly. Chester was keen but had to convince his father it was the right move. At the time there were only two restaurants attached to vineyards and wineries in McLaren Vale. With more than 65 per cent of their produce exported overseas, d'Arenberg's financial future looked secure, so the investment was made.

The original homestead, built by the Miltons in the 1880s and first occupied by Frank in 1912, was renovated and extended to include a restaurant in 1996. Chester and d'Arry happily made their application to the Onkaparinga Council to renovate, but by the time they realised they had applied only to build a verandah, they had already appointed a chef who was planning restaurant menus. They had to resubmit their application for a permit for a commercial kitchen and a new cellar door building. Approval was eventually given and the restaurant and cellar door constructed. As it was the new verandah that initially received planning permission, the new restaurant was named 'd'Arry's Verandah'. The cellar door is beside the enclosed dining terrace.

Initially leased by Andrew Scott Davies, the restaurant became an instant success and received accolades as the best vineyard restaurant in South Australia. However, this initial venture was soon dissolved and Andrew Davies moved to another premises. The next partnership was with Pip and Michael Ewers. Although their food was popular, as a financial venture it was unsuccessful, so Chester and d'Arry searched for another business partner. Since 2004 the restaurant has been run by the partnership of Jo and Peter Reschke and Nigel Rich. This combination works well for both d'Arenberg and diners. The food is very popular and the restaurant is full every day. It continues to be praised for its ambience and the innovative and imaginative use of local produce, and has been described as 'a winter bolt hole … amongst twisted gums with broad valley views over vineyards to the ranges beyond'. The September 2011 edition of *Australian Gourmet Traveller* highlights the fact that the wine produced at d'Arenberg 'inspires the menu'. However, it is the 'intelligent use of local produce' that defines the dishes:

> *Lush extravagance defines blue swimmer crab and prawn ravioli with lobster medallion and bisque. Generous serves characterise the eight options for entrée and mains, three cheeses and seven deserts — many spiked with d'Arenberg wines, the mainstays of a list augmented by several classy imports.*[45]

On the marriage of old and new combinations of wine and food, this review points to the very nature and philosophy of the winery and vineyard. It takes as its starting point the old ingredients — grape varieties and food — and mixes them with the new and contemporary ideas. d'Arry takes great pride in the restaurant bearing his name.

One major award bestowed on Chester in 1996 of which he is particularly proud, especially as it was awarded on the eve of the birth of his first child, was the Hyatt/Advertiser 'South Australian Wine of the Year Award'. The award was won in the Shiraz category for the Dead Arm Shiraz 1994, but d'Arenberg were also runners-up for the Noble Riesling 1994 in the Sweet Wines category. The wine's origin, the disease that created the 'dead arm' of the Dead Arm, was then adopted as an advertising theme for the wine and the award.

More land — and more taxes

A year after the restaurant was launched, in 1997 the Osborn partnership made its first major purchase of land since 1958. For years the McLaren Vale winemaking district had been threatened by land sales for housing — the inevitable encroachment of developers who saw the Vale, just 40 minutes from Adelaide, as prime real estate. In June 1997 the property known as 'Russell's Farm' was offered for sale. This land had been in the hands of David and Sue Russell and their family since early in the century. d'Arry understood a developer had already earmarked the block for subdivision. Although he clearly wanted more land to extend the vineyard's capacity, his commitment to McLaren Vale and his objection to the insidious invasion of developers must have played a part in his decision. This view was supported by a McLaren Vale real estate agent who commented that d'Arenberg's purchase 'created a precedent in the region for land sales' and protected one of the state's 'most historic and lucrative viticultural regions from housing encroachment'.[46] The property of 103 acres runs between Kangarilla Road and Chalk Hill Road in between McLaren Vale and McLaren Flat. It falls under the jurisdiction of two district councils, however, and the purchase took seven months to negotiate. On its north-western boundary it adjoins the vineyards of Sir Dennis Patterson. Although once described as 'a flagon's throw' across the road from d'Arenberg's original vineyard, it is in fact much further down the hill. The gently sloping flat plains straddle Peddler's Creek, a fast-running winter watercourse that drops from the Willunga Escarpment to the sea at Moana.[47] When purchased, it was planted to an almond grove. It was decided to name the new property 'Peddler's Divide' because it straddles the two sides of the creek. The block now has 88.5 acres of planted vines.

Although this was the first purchase of land for 40 years, d'Arry has made it clear over the intervening years that he 'rued not purchasing adjoining property in the hills north of McLaren Vale' on the rare occasions when they became available. Although an astute businessman, we can only conclude that his natural caution when spending money influenced his previous decision making. The company paid $20 000 per hectare for the Russell land, making it a purchase of more than $1 million. The land had been planted with vines producing 'reasonable good yields' until 1978. It would now be used to plant three white Rhône varieties,

Viognier, Marsanne and Rousanne, among others. This purchase allowed Chester and d'Arry to double their production to 260 000 cases per annum, a large percentage of this volume being earmarked for export.[48]

Death and taxes, we know, are the only certainties in life. The Australian wine industry, in the past 20 or more years, has faced horrendous levels of taxation. Winemakers' profitability, first hit by a 12 per cent state licence fee and the imposition of a 10 per cent sales tax in 1984, increased to 20 per cent in 1986, was further reduced by the 1993 tax of 41 per cent. When it was decided by the Howard Coalition government in 1999 to impose a 10 per cent goods and services tax, a revision of wine taxation was undertaken. With his father, Chester took part in the discussions and remembers the day very well:

> *The WET tax was decided here [at d'Arry's Verandah]. John Howard came down here for lunch when they were working out what they were going to do with the GST. They were going to have some sort of* ad valorum *tax like a sort of excise-based tax. The Wine Federation, which was represented mainly by the big companies, didn't want that at all, because it would make cheap wine very expensive and expensive wine cheap and they wanted the status quo, so they set up a lunch here. It was $1000 a ticket and there were about 16 people, and John came along and I sat in on that one as well and there were a few farmers, rich farmers, who wanted to come along and hear what was going on ... and we told him there and then, it was Ian Sutton from the Wine Federation [who] put forward that we didn't want this tax clearly, and we had the support of the industry. He listened and he said okay, fair enough, and went and came up with the Wine Equalisation*

Tax (WET). But ... we didn't know how much the Wine Equalisation Tax was going to be, and when he ... actually came out with 29 per cent we said 'well it's actually higher than it was before', because when you put the 10 per cent on top of the 29 per cent (in a restaurant, for instance, it goes up to 40-odd per cent whereas a bottle shop it's 41 or so), but the outcome is that the tax has actually gone up on wine. So the government said, 'Well we'll give the first $1 million worth of sales of each winery, we'll give them WET exemption'. So in other words they got $290000 or something back on every $1 million, and then they even increased that to $1½ million, so it's roughly $500000 you get back now.[49]

Australia's wine companies, large and small, have found ways to deal with this tax ever since.

Chester soars

Chester began accumulating awards as early as 1984, so winning prizes was not new to him, but from the late 1990s they were snowballing. In 1998 he became *Winestate* magazine's inaugural 'Winemaker of the Year'. The following year d'Arenberg won the Wine Society Perpetual Trophy for the 'Most Successful Winery of the Competition' at the Sydney International 'Top 100' Competition. In 1999, 2007 and 2011 d'Arenberg was named by *Wine & Spirits Magazine* in the United States as one of their 'Australian Wineries of the Year'. In 2004 d'Arenberg won the inaugural Len Evans Memorial Trophy at the UK International Wine

Challenge for the most consistent winery over five years. The following year, 2005, Chester was named 'Wine Personality of the Year' in Robert Parker Junior's Wine Advocate. He was also chosen by the Australian Wine Selectors as the 'Winemaker of the Year' and the top 'Shining Light' of the Australian wine industry, and to top off the year, his entry of the Dead Arm Shiraz was recognised in Langton's Wine Classification 'Australia's Top 101 Wines' as 'Excellent'.

As chief winemaker, he was experimenting with grape varieties old and new. Most, but not all, of Chester's experiments worked and went on to become successful labels. But wine tastes, as we know, can be fickle and influenced by fashion. Chester talked recently about one of his unsuccessful experiments. In 2001 he made a Nebbiolo that was very difficult to sell because of its very tannic grape quality. According to Halliday, it is 'universally accepted as the greatest or most noble of the many hundreds of Italian red grape varieties'. It has an ancient history and is grown in Piedmont, where the great Barolos and Barbarescos are made from this variety alone.[50] In Australia the oldest plantings of Nebbiolo and Barbera are at Montrose in Mudgee, where vines date back to the 1980s. In the McLaren Vale, Halliday rates Coriole the best producer of this variety. Having fun with the Italian wine variety Barbaresco, Chester called his bottled variety the 'Barbara Says So'. The back label told the story that his daughters 'don't do as they're told and they're taking directives from Barbie dolls, and hence Barbara Says So'. Despite the amusing name, people in the tasting room didn't take to it, preferring other styles, and d'Arenberg ended up selling it all to the Wine Society in England about three years later. 'They bought the lot and they were quite impressed with it.' Looking back on it, Chester thinks 'it was starting to look quite interesting actually at that stage'.[51] We wonder how it would work now.

Chardonnay and Mourvèdre have both been successfully grown at d'Arenberg. In recent years, they have been grafting quite a lot of Chardonnay to other varieties, especially Mourvèdre. In 'The House' vineyard, which was nearly 100 years old, Mourvèdre was pulled out in 1979 and Chardonnay was planted in 1980 for the Chardonnay boom of the 1980s. This particular vineyard is a shallow red earth on limestone, and it was quite difficult for Chardonnay to produce the way Chester wanted it to; it was 'lower yielding than other vineyards, 'a bit too open, a bit forward, because of the warmer site'. Instead, Chester grafted the Chardonnay back to Mourvèdre again, 'so it's good fine Mourvèdre again'.[52]

The export market — flagship wines find a niche

d'Arenberg have been exporting high volumes of wine since the 1980s. d'Arry recalls when they initially managed to sell their wine to an agent in The Netherlands:

> *The first bit of export really came about through Albert Heine, from the Netherlands, coming out and they were looking for cheap wine for their supermarkets. And they looked at our bottled wine. They were pretty big, our wines, and they weren't used to them overseas at all at that stage. They didn't like the bottled wines much; and then he tried our cask wine and he said, 'Oh, that's lovely. Could we have some of that?'*[53]

Chester recalls:

That night we had dinner, I remember I was discussing the Bordeaux vintages 1982 and 1983 with the buyer — which was better — and Dad said, 'You argued with him all night, he won't buy anything now'. Well, he did.[54]

With the bleak outlook for the domestic market at the time, both Chester and d'Arry were thrilled with the acceptance of their Shiraz and Shiraz/Grenache blend into the Netherlands. They were one of very few companies successfully exporting to Europe then.

In London in 1985 Hazel Murphy had taken up the challenge of importing Australian wine into the United Kingdom. Her Australia Day tastings became legendary, and had the desired effect. 'Brand Australia' was launched into a market eager to try the big bold wines from the antipodes, which were preferred over the French and Bulgarian wines of poor quality and a certain snob value. In 1986 the wine chain Oddbins provided a breakthrough for Australian wines. Those new to wine drinking now sought out the fruity style disparaged by the previous generation of British drinkers of Australian wine. One of the younger wine writers in England, Jane Macquitty, wrote a glowing article in the London *Times* in 1986, praising the wines being sold for £2.69 and asking the obvious question: how could wine from Australia be shipped and sold at this price and make a profit? The reality, of course, was that the Australian producers could not afford to sell at this price. Rather than making a profit at the time, they probably used these wines as 'loss leaders' while educating the British about the different

Australian regions and styles. In time they would prove to be profitable lines for the Australian companies. This article is said to have had an immediate effect on sales, and within a year Oddbins' sales amounted to hundreds of thousands of cases. The small chain retained the market for Australian wine for two years before the supermarket chains also began importing cheap, usually good-quality Australian wine.

In 1987 Chester decided to go upmarket in their wine pricing. At that stage they were selling for just under $10 per bottle, but he now priced them at $14 or $15. Some thought it would kill the brand, d'Arry recalls, but it didn't — sales went up immediately, and retailers told him he had previously undervalued the product. Hazel Murphy advised him that d'Arenberg needed to get into the £3 market because that was where the sales were. Instead, he said that they wanted to get into the £8 market, where the profit and quality was. Hazel later told him he was right, because the bottom market was vulnerable to the Argentinians and others at that time. 'And of course Southcorp buggered the whole market up in England by discounting like crazy; suddenly it wasn't distinctive wine any more, it was cheap wine.'[55]

By the mid 1990s growth in exports had reached unprecedented levels and international sales formed a larger proportion of Australian production than in the peak period before the Second World War. As d'Arry stressed at the time, 'we' — Australia in general and d'Arenberg in particular — needed strong export markets. In the mid 1980s d'Arenberg were exporting approximately 50 per cent of their product overseas; a decade later it was about 65 per cent. In 2010 d'Arry proudly boasted: 'We won the Exporters Award I think because we've got so many countries — 65 countries — and we're probably 70 per cent export I think'.[56] Exports account for more than half of d'Arenberg's market. But to maintain their market share, they needed greater volumes of produce. It had been 10 years since the last major purchase of land, and the year 2007 marked the acquisition of four new vineyards.

The Mustard Block, on the corner of Tatachilla and California roads, was the first acquisition. Of the total 80 acres, 72 acres are planted with Shiraz, Cabernet Sauvignon, Grenache, Merlot, Petit Verdot, Temperanillo, Tinto Cao, Verdhelho and Viognier. The next purchase was a vineyard of 48 acres named Little Venice. Located on the corner of Kays and Foggo roads, it is planted with 18 acres of Shiraz. The Edge Vineyard in Douglas Gully Road is of 82.75 acres, with 40 planted with a variety of mainly red grapes. Finally, in December, Bamboo Ridge on Whitings Road was purchased. This block of 55.1 acres has 48.1 acres planted with Merlot, Chardonnay, Shiraz, Chenin Blanc, Petit Verdot, Semillon and Cabernet. The following year saw two further purchases of land. The Wilcadene and Sunrise vineyards, together consisting of just over 30 acres, are now planted with mainly red varieties such as Cinsault, Grenache, Shiraz and Cabernet Sauvignon.

By 2010 and 2011 d'Arenberg's production had expanded dramatically over previous decades. They now process approximately 4800 tonnes of grapes each year.

Yet with the fickleness of the Australian consumer and world markets, not to mention uncertainties in national and international politics and the economy, d'Arry, Chester and other family winemakers all felt an independent marketing initiative for Australian wines was needed.

d'Arenberg: proudly one of Australia's First Families of Wine

The story of Australian wine growing, production and marketing over the past 150 years has been defined by a small number of large producers and a large number of small producers. The export of Australian wine has been and will remain inextricably linked to the history and survival of the Australian wine industry. But as we have seen through the story of one winery, it is not that simple. The fortunes or otherwise of those in the industry are determined to varying degrees by internal Australian social, political and economic factors. They also depend on international alliances and the value of the Australian dollar. The wine industry, much like the mining industry, is subject to 'boom and bust' cycles, and to date we can track five major booms. Australian wine drinkers can be fickle. In simple terms, wine tastes are determined by fashion — Sauvignon Blanc versus Riesling or Chardonnay, Shiraz versus Grenache or Pinot Noir, and so on. Booms and busts have come and gone, and governments and the major wine industry bodies have not always supported the smaller producers in the way they would have hoped.

In July 2006 winemakers from 12 of Australia's intergenerational winemaking families met before Wine Australia in Sydney. Alister Purbrick instigated the meeting to bring together the skill, talent and enormous wealth of experience of the wine families. For three years they worked towards establishing a collective. Promoting themselves as the 'heart and soul of Australian wine', Australia's First Families of Wine aimed to engage consumers, retailers, restaurateurs and industry members across the globe and to educate them about the character of the winemakers and their wines. The members of the inaugural group were: Brown Brothers (established 1885), Campbells (1870), d'Arenberg (1912), De Bortoli (1928), Henschke (1868), Howard Park (the Burch family) (1986), Jim Barry Wines (1959), McWilliams (1877), Tahbilk (the Purbrick family) (1860), and Taylors (1969). Membership depended on satisfying the following criteria:

- being family controlled, as defined under the Australian Corporations Act
- having a history of at least two (preferably three) generations involved in the business
- the ability to offer a tasting of at least 20 vintages of one or more iconic brands
- membership of the Winemakers' Federation of Australia
- ownership of established vineyards more than 50 years old and/or distinguished sites that exemplify the best of terroir
- a commitment to environmental best practice in vineyards, wineries and packaging
- family-member service on wine industry bodies
- a long-term commitment to export markets.

The collective was officially launched by the then Federal Minister for Agriculture, Fisheries and Forestry, Tony Burke, MP, at a gala event at the Sydney Opera House on 31 August 2009. The Australia's First Families of Wine (AFFW) 'put some colour, life and movement from a family perspective back into an Australian wine scene dominated by the big corporates'.[57] d'Arenberg Wines, who could satisfactorily demonstrate their ability to meet all these criteria, have become a valued member of this group. Chester and d'Arry travel overseas frequently to promote both the AFFW and their own wines.

Chester is enthusiastic when discussing d'Arenberg's involvement with the AFFW. The collective approach to marketing premium Australian wines overseas is of enormous benefit to all the families. They have great fun when they travel overseas to market their wine, and most families now have the next generation — 'children' in their twenties and thirties — already working with them. Chester's children are too young yet, but it appears that his youngest daughter, Mia, aged eight, is already keen to follow the family tradition. The Australian government provides a significant financial benefit in the form of a marketing grant for the 12 families. They meet with great success in England and Canada as well as France and the United States; in 2012 they will forge their way into Asia. The collective is not just about the bargaining power of the great wine families working as a conglomerate to market their wine. It is also about the camaraderie and fun, and the personal and business links being made internationally demonstrate the value of the financial outlay required to become a member of this collective.[58]

Making old-world wines in the new world

Looking back on Chester's 27 years as chief winemaker, a handful of milestone events stand out, helping to explain why d'Arenberg has reached its level of national and international success.

Chester, the university-educated winemaker, went somewhat against expectations when he returned home to make wine for himself. Rather than simply embracing new technologies and leaving the ancient traditions behind, he gradually introduced old-world, labour-intensive, methods of winemaking. In blending the old with the new, he also began to incorporate current thinking and modern, practical technologies. He began in 1984 by putting in more refrigeration for white wine production and using more new oak barrels. This, he believes, dramatically added to the style and elegance of the wines. Refrigeration was further increased in 1987. His pride and joy, it must be said, was the purchase of the open-mouthed, rubber-toothed Demoisy crusher in 1989 to replace the Whitehill beater crusher used for more than 30 years. This meant the grapes are crushed using a much gentler process. The grapes are not as damaged, the whole berry is not crushed or beaten to a pulp, so the wine is less bitter and more fragrant. The 'Lucky Lizard' Chardonnay was named for the bearded dragon lizards that like to sun themselves on the vineyard posts and watch for prey. Sometimes they are dislodged and find their way into a load of grapes destined for the winery, but the very gentle Demoisy crusher allows them to pass through the ordeal slightly shaken but otherwise unharmed!

By 1997 Chester had stopped fertilising the vineyards and was achieving great results. He went to great lengths to eliminate any trace of stalks, which tend to impart a 'hay flavour' to the wine; removal of the stalks gives a purer flavour. In 1998 he started buying large volumes of oak, which also enhance the flavours and style of the wine. d'Arenberg have also worked on how to get the most out of wine with submerged caps — that is, with the skins held down in the juice during fermentation. In 2000 Chester returned to the ancient practice of foot treading the wine. This assists with extraction, helps cool the skins down and gives a further elegance to the final product.

d'Arenberg's use of open fermentation, foot treading and basket pressing to preserve primary fruit characters creates structured wines that age well. In the early 2000s they began assessing the use of Stelvin caps. A selection of red wines from the 2002 and 2003 vintages were sealed with screw caps to assess their performance against cork on their wines. According to Chester, 'Each wine showed more fruit on the nose and had a sweeter mid-palate. At no stage did they look hard or raw. The tannins still softened as normal ageing took place and we did not find any sign of oxidisation or woody cork like aromas or flavours as were evident on some of the cork sealed bottles'.[59] Since the 2004 vintage all d'Arenberg wines made for sale in Australia, the United Kingdom and New Zealand have been sealed with screw caps. In 2004 Chester also gave up racking the red wines; that is, instead of pumping wine out of barrels several times he chose to leave the wine with the skins on for the entire period of barrel maturation. This practice acts as an antioxidant.

The latest innovation in wine production has been the introduction of single vineyard and single district wines. Small parcels of grapes from some of the best sites have been made into wine that would normally be incorporated into the icon wines. Instead they have been set aside for wines that will be a part of the centenary celebrations in 2012.

Chester Osborn has been described as a winemaker who 'tastes' wine differently from other Australian winemakers. He has been buying European wine for many

years now and he believes his palate has become attuned to the European style rather than the 'bigger, fatter [Australian] wines with their earth characters'.[60] The change may have happened incrementally over the years as well. Is it really a change in style, though? It may have always have been there in d'Arenberg wines, beginning when Frank Osborn blended Shiraz and Grenache to produce the first Bundarra Vineyards Burgundy for sale in bulk and in bottles back in 1928. At the time, this was a popular style of wine for the overseas market. The style was continued by d'Arry when he began bottling his own wine in 1959. As we have learned, fashion also influences style and it is now more fashionable to enjoy the European style and grape varieties. Certainly d'Arenberg's export market demands this style; according to Chester, it is a style they can relate to much more than the bigger, fruitier Australian red wines. Chester travels overseas three times each year and engages directly with agents, buyers and individual wine lovers. For some time now d'Arenberg has been a truly international brand.

Celebrating 100 years

In December 1911, when Joseph and Frank Osborn signed the sale note to purchase the Milton property, they were eager to make a life as grape growers in the McLaren Vale region. Frank enthusiastically embraced the vineyard in 1912 because he had a strong desire to go onto the land as a farmer; he also fancied himself as a 'vigneron'. After more than a dozen years of learning how to grow grapes, Frank proved himself as a vigneron when he began producing his own wine. In those early years McLaren Vale produced grapes that were sold to the overseas market or made into sweet red wines or brandy. When he began to make his own wine, a burgundy and a sweet red, he had help from his neighbours, particularly Cud Kay of Kay Brothers. In the late 1920s Bundarra Vineyards was one of a handful of wineries and vineyards located in McLaren Vale; this did not change until the 1960s and 1970s. In 1957, when Frank Osborn died, his youngest son, d'Arry, became the third-generation winemaker. d'Arry learned to make wine 'by the seat of his pants'; luckily he had a natural aptitude for the art. Within two years he had created his own label, naming it after his mother, Helen d'Arenberg.

The now famous 'd'Arenberg' label, whose red stripe and coat of arms have their own stories to tell, is recognised around the world. Despite changing wine tastes, the original blend of Grenache and Shiraz grapes continues to be produced as d'Arry's Original Shiraz Grenache and remains as popular today as it was when it was first attracting attention in the late 1960s. The most successful early Grenache Shiraz blend was the 1969 Burgundy, which won 29 gold medals, 7 trophies and 49 awards.

McLaren Vale is famous for both its white and red varieties, and d'Arenberg has played its part in this celebrity, producing a portfolio of 45 memorable wines (at last count), each with its own quirky name and story. Chester Osborn, fourth-generation vigneron, viticulturalist and current chief winemaker, took over at a time when popular tastes in wine were changing dramatically. Wine drinkers and critics alike were calling for new, fruitier styles, and these are what Chester began to experiment with. He introduced new technology while keeping faith with old and tested techniques. His unusual combinations of grape varieties and innovative

methods have garnered him many prestigious winemaking awards over the years. Today d'Arenberg Wines produces 355 000 cases a year and has a turnover of $26 million, with 140 staff working at the winery. d'Arenberg continues to produce its iconic wines and to develop new and creative blends of obscure and untried grape varieties. Chester Osborn is known for successfully pushing the boundaries. As d'Arenberg wines continue to resonate 'across the undulating and peaceful landscape of McLaren Vale', their reach is ever wider.[61] After one hundred years, the distinctive red stripe of the d'Arenberg label is recognised, the name respected and admired, in the old winemaking world and the new.

Notes from the winemaker

by Chester Osborn

CHESTER OSBORN HAS BEEN AT THE WINEMAKING HELM AT D'ARENBERG SINCE 1983. The techniques he employs in the vineyard and winery are a culmination of experience and the lessons he has learned from his predecessors. Rather than conform to a philosophy or pre-existing regime, Chester has formed his own method through experimentation, a carefully honed palate and an insistence on small-batch winemaking, which allows him to follow vineyards vintage to vintage.

In the following pages Chester shares his insights into viticulture, where he takes a minimal and natural approach, putting grape quality ahead of yields in search of an uncompromised expression of the vineyard. This method recalls the way grapes were grown at the start of the d'Arenberg journey, before the use of tractors, fertilisers and irrigation.

Vineyard minimal input

Lately organic and biodynamic viticulture has been well publicised and widely adopted. From the late 1990s d'Arenberg has been practising what I consider to be the next extension from these two practices, which I refer to as minimal input.

171

Organic and biodynamic grape growing can include considerable fertilisation and irrigation; however, our minimal input philosophy demands no use of fertilisers and minimal or no irrigation. If irrigation is required, it is only at strategic times. These times include winter, to imitate natural rainfall in drier years, or in early spring or late December, after grape cell division and enlargement is complete.

In my opinion, the application of nitrogen-based fertiliser and excessive irrigation produce grapes grown in an environment similar to hydroponics. It is my belief that the mineral tannin and much of the character of the wine comes from the soil and makes up the soil flavour. Minimal input growing encourages vines to explore the whole soil root volume, spreading wider and deeper into the soil. As a result, the vine gets all its nutrients from the soil, which enhances the characters unique to that particular site. The resultant wine is bigger and richer, the ripening is more gradual, and heat and disease resistance is increased. I have also found that the wines made from these vineyards age longer.

Non-cultivation of the soil is another key element of our minimal input philosophy. In my experience, cultivation slowly sterilises the soil. Every time cultivation occurs a new population of aerobic bacteria grows on the recently introduced carbon matter. This effectively eats the existing nutrients and the newly introduced oxygen and overpowers the anaerobic bacteria. When these food sources are depleted the population largely dies, having leeched the anaerobic bacteria from the soil. We have found that continual cultivation not only destroys soil structure but will gradually produce an environment that is not conducive to growing vines. By not cultivating and mowing only when water conservation is required, the roots break down gradually, continually adding carbon and oxygen to the soil. This produces a more consistent environment with a stable population of organisms, an environment favourable to the vines. The additional microflora increase the water-holding capacity of the soil and the root holes assist in water penetration, both aiding water conservation and reducing the need for irrigation.

I also strongly believe that a minimal input approach is very sustainable for the soil. In our experience, the addition of charged fertilisers over time remove elements and micronutrients from the soil. The vines use only some of the fertiliser compounds, while the excess attach to soil elements for later use. Some are also washed through the soil during heavy periods of rain, eventually finding their way to an underground aquifer and possibly polluting it. It stands to reason that after years of fertiliser application the soil will be depleted of certain useful elements. These elements are useful for building minerality and earth complexity into grapes, and therefore into wine. To manually add these elements (for example, as ground-up granite) is possible, but it's expensive and less effective; it will result in alternative grape flavours and therefore will make a different wine.

All of these effects on the soil also apply to the geology. It takes some time for nitrogen to be depleted from the soil and improve the grape quality. The deeper the soil/geology available to the vine, the longer it takes to bring the fertility to a stable level. The time period can be from a year or two to over a decade, depending on the conditions.

I believe there is a misconception regarding the amount of nitrogen required to grow grapes. Levels of soil fertility recommended by fertiliser companies generally do not support the production of high-quality grapes, in my opinion. Grapes contain very little protein (a major group of compounds incorporating

much of the nitrogen). It is true that some of the many hundreds of different compounds found in grapes/wine possibly do have nitrogen associated. However, many of these compounds can have a negative effect on the balance of characters, masking or altering the final character of the wine. From my experience, the soil and geology that can sustain low nitrogen levels, economically yielding grapes from vines with the correct balanced amount of vigour, will produce grapes — and therefore wine — of superior quality.

Recent soil/root interaction research has shown that if the nitrogen level is low the root will behave in a quite different manner. The enzymatic reactions used to absorb nutrients behave quite differently under fertilised conditions, which I imagine is the reason why grapes from unfertilised vines have more expression of the soil.

Grape vines have undergone many thousands of years of genetic alteration through natural selection to create perfect grapes that will attract birds and animals ahead of those of a neighbouring vine. Based on the assumption that birds and animals favour the most flavourful and mineral grapes, and as vines were not fertilised before human intervention, it follows that unfertilised vines will make the best grapes. Tannins and acidity in grapes may have developed partly to reduce the sweet, cloying taste effect but also to increase disease resistance. Animals and birds would not eat less tasty or diseased grapes, which would therefore not be spread with the droppings for propagation. With human interaction fungicide sprays can overcome spoiled moulds like botrytis, but the grapes from fertilised vines will still be inferior tasting.

We have noticed that grapes grown without fertiliser have thicker skins and more turgid berries with increased natural disease resistance from increased tannin levels. I believe these effects can be measured through the ratio of nitrogen to micronutrients. The lower the ratio, the higher the grape flavour, quality and disease resistance. Yields don't necessarily suffer. The quality of the grapes is usually at least doubled (and often lifted much higher), producing grapes that contribute to wines selling at between $29 and $65 instead of $10 to $18 or lower.

It is my experience that wines made from minimal input vineyards behave similarly to some of the best European wines, with more soil character and tightness, length and age ability. I strongly believe it is a style that Australia should be making more of, as it will help tell the story of regionality and ultimately assist in making more refined, high-end wines. I have always aimed for a style that tastes somewhere between Australian and European wines, having the best of both worlds. This requires of the European wine consumer, and those with a preference for this style, less adjustment from their normal drinking habits. I believe this style has been a pivotal factor in establishing d'Arenberg's fine wine reputation and has been vital to its acceptance in over 60 countries.

Tools of vine balance adjustment

Low grape yield is often mentioned as a prerequisite for making great wine. I believe its importance is overstated, however, and tells only a part of the story.

A grape vine is self-adjusting and capable of surviving without human interaction. I have made wines that I am very proud of from derelict vines not pruned for over 25 years, including The Derelict Vineyard Grenache. The grapes from these vines truly express the site better than any other growing practice would. It is through working with these vines in the early 1990s that I came to hone the minimal input viticulture system we now use across d'Arenberg's vineyards. Many vineyards were left to their own devices following the government's effort to reduce the surplus of grapes. The vine pull scheme of 1986 paid growers to pull out vines. Some growers accepted the money but left the vines to wither away rather than pulling them from the ground because it was the cheaper option. In hindsight, government support might have been more usefully channelled into export assistance, as the scheme was introduced only just before the huge export boom that started around 1989.

My mother always taught me, out of everything bad that happens twice as much good will occur. This is something I have always believed in. In 1992 a Grenache grower of ours with near derelict vines that were producing amazing grapes sold the vineyard. The new owner decided to sell the grapes to a different winery. This prompted me to put an ad in *Grapegrower & Winemaker* magazine offering twice the price for small berry, dry grown McLaren Vale bush vine Grenache: we offered $1000 per tonne, which caused quite an uproar amongst wineries as it talked up the price of grapes. Before this there had been only a small variance in grape prices based on quality within a variety. (It was and remains my view that higher quality grapes should achieve a much higher price. Today grape prices vary enormously based on quality.) As a result, d'Arenberg ended up with access to many of these vineyards, and this is how the minimal input approach to viticulture at d'Arenberg was born.

This relates to vine balance because in a fertiliser-free and minimally irrigated vine, the above-ground parts reflect the below-ground parts. Putting it simply, a deep, high water-holding soil/geology will have a big root system and produce vines of higher vigour. The reverse applies for shallow soils with less access to water. Human interaction interferes with this and, in turn, the resulting grapes. When we practise minimal input viticulture (no fertiliser, no cultivation, no herbicide, no or nearly no irrigation), we rely largely on only the trellis system and pruning technique as the tools of adjustment.

By working with the previously mentioned derelict vineyards we have noticed that the vine adjusts its yield per shoot and the number of shoots to its pruning level. The more buds that are left, the higher the percentage of dormant buds will remain in a season. The vine pushes the number of buds it can safely ripen. It should be noted that this regulation is not as evident in young vines and can result in overcropping with them. The number of set grapes and the size of the berry are also determined by the vine's root system and history. The shoot length is reduced if there are more shoots. What is important is the leaf area to fruit weight ratio, as the leaves ripen the grapes. Based on this understanding we can largely prune to any bud level and as long as we continue to prune to that level, the vine will crop to the amount it can ripen. However, the grapes will make quite different wines at different pruning levels. The vines with more buds produce small, exposed berries with high tannin levels. This may be good in a cold year, as less tannin is often seen in cold years and more exposure will increase tannin level. In hot years, however, increased exposure will greatly decrease fruit characters. So depending on the variety and its natural tannin content, we need to adjust the pruning level to achieve the desired balance between fruit and tannin. Grenache can grow from vines with huge bud numbers, as it is a low tannin variety. Shiraz and Cabernet can be grown with reasonably high bud numbers, while Aglianico, Nebbiollo and Sagrantino need low bud numbers because of the high tannin levels.

There is yet another layer of complexity, because the trellis system also plays a significant role in the equation. A single cordon will be more shaded and produce a fruitier wine with less tannin than a spread-out high double cordon trellis. So a single cordon trellis is good for the hot years while the latter is better for the cold years. I do not believe in vertical shoot positioning in McLaren Vale, as clumps of leaves overshade each other as well as fruit. Mottled light here seems to work better than either direct sunlight or full shade.

Another consideration in the search for vine balance is the soil and geology. Sands generally produce wines with the emphasis on fruit flowers and less tannin, while clays over calcareous geology express a lot of tannin. In a hotter year the sand-based vineyards will produce a good balance of fruit and tannin, which can be adjusted via trellis methods and pruning level. In a cold, wet year they let in more water and produce wines with lower tannin levels. The higher trellis on clay/loam over calcium carbonate in the cold, wet years has a good balance between fruit and tannins, while the reverse applies for hot, dry years.

If the desire is for consistency, the best results will be achieved by growing vines on various different soils and geology on different trellis systems with slightly different pruning regimes on each. In cool years different amounts of different vineyards will go into the blend as compared with hot years. The year will always shine through to a certain degree but this can be modified, or we can make wines that reflect the years perfectly. The choice is in the hands of the winemaker.

The football-shaped image in figure 1 illustrates the enormous effects of nitrogen fertiliser, fertility of sites and heat on the growing environment.

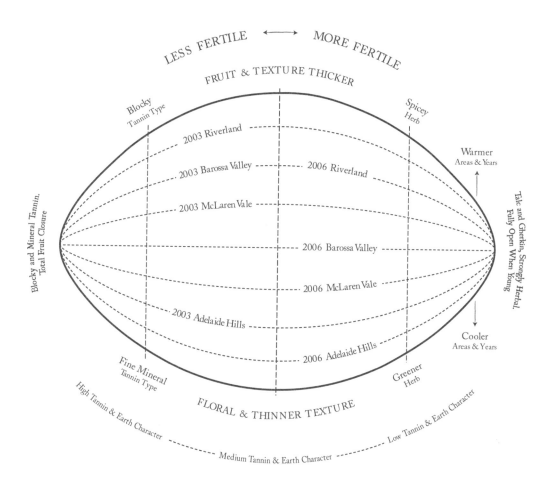

LESS FERTILE ↔ MORE FERTILE

FRUIT & TEXTURE THICKER

Blocky
Tannin Type

Spicey
Herb

Warmer
Areas & Years

Blocky and Mineral Tannin.
Total Fruit Closure

2003 Riverland

2003 Barossa Valley — — — — 2006 Riverland

2003 McLaren Vale

Talc and Gherkin, Strongly Herbal.
Fully Open When Young

2006 Barossa Valley

2006 McLaren Vale

2003 Adelaide Hills

Cooler
Areas & Years

Fine Mineral
Tannin Type

2006 Adelaide Hills

Greener
Herb

FLORAL & THINNER TEXTURE

High Tannin & Earth Character

Low Tannin & Earth Character

Medium Tannin & Earth Character

Figure 1: The wine football hacker

Notes and assumptions

- Lines with indicated areas and years are an average of many sites in an area in a year.
- The mid fertility point in today's fertilised world is a relatively low fertile point.
- Irrigation is restricted (not in excess and not causing undue stress).
- The same winemaking method is used for each plot.
- The variables discussed in the previous pages — trellis, pruning and soil/geology — will influence where the resultant wine lies on the chart.
- Sugar, flavour and tannin ripeness is achieved without overripening.

Here we can plot a big or small spot that best describes the wine. Green, hard tannins can still be seen in the wines from highly fertilised vines; however, even if sugar ripe or flavour ripe, these grapes are not tannin ripe.

Extremely gentle winemaking

The d'Arenberg winery during vintage recalls a bygone area, with purple-stained cellar hands performing manual tasks such as foot treading and ferment digs. While many wineries have adopted new technology in search of economic efficiency, Chester has structured his winemaking processes around wine quality. At the core of his philosophy is gentle handling and maintaining small batches all the way through the process. Small batches are essential for gaining and developing an understanding of individual vineyards, a critical component in Chester's quest to make great wine.

Through constant refinement of the processes involved and continual experimentation, Chester has developed unique solutions in the winery. He has insisted on using time-honoured techniques such as foot treading, open fermentation and basket pressing, making them economically viable through innovative thinking. This unique approach has been fundamental in creating and maintaining the soulful style evident in all Chester's wines, from the humble Stump Jump range to one of Australia's iconic reds, The Dead Arm.

In the following pages Chester discusses some of these innovations and shares his opinions on a range of winemaking topics.

Winemaking at d'Arenberg involves utilising modified old-fashioned equipment in conjunction with new technology. The process starts with crushing. An old, aggressive Whitehill beater crusher was replaced with a gentle Demoisy crusher in 1989, and more recently a modified Velo model. This investment was made to achieve soft crushing with higher throughput and versatility. The aim is to remove the grapes from the stalks and keep as many berries whole as possible. Whole berries amplify fragrance and elegance, which is often a good thing in big ripe reds from McLaren Vale. In some instances, less whole berries may be desired and can be achieved by closing the rollers. If the year is cold and the parcel is therefore elegant, it is often better to have less whole berries to increase the weight and possibly, but not necessarily, the tannins.

The resultant must (grape juice, skins and seeds) should also be free of matter other than grapes. Modifications to the Velo crusher involved replacing hard de-stemming fingers with softer rubber fingers and reducing the size of the holes in the cage in order to keep as many whole berries as possible. The ferments needed to be small enough to be mobile so they could be put next to the crusher, reducing pump friction and the need to crush berries. The old-fashioned concrete submerged cap, stone, open fermenters were copied in size and effective working design and then made out of stainless steel so they could be mobile. When full, the stainless steel fermenters are stored in insulated sheds with large doors that can be opened to make the most of natural temperatures and reduce the need for manual heating or cooling. The fermenters have many advantages over the old concrete fermenters:

- They are moveable, allowing for whole berry inclusion.
- They are heated easily by placing in the sun or by gas Spitfire-style heaters.
- They are efficiently cooled by opening the shed or pulling the fermenters out in cooler weather.
- They are easily and gently emptied by a spinning head forklift, removing the need for aggressive augers or expensive manual handling.

Many vineyards stopped using open fermenters because of the associated Occupational Health and Safety issues. But the stainless steel mobile open fermenters overcome most of these problems. Open fermenters in Australia largely gave way to larger tank fermenters because winemakers believed the process would become more efficient. However, our own economic analysis indicates that this slightly more labour-intensive process is more cost effective because there is less capital outlay. From a winemaking perspective, smaller parcels of fruit can be kept separate, allowing more flexibility and finetuning of blends. The fermenters also went out of popularity because the cap often got too hot and colour and flavour extraction was insufficient. However, when harvesting by night, when grapes are 12 to 18°C, the cap never gets uncomfortably hot. The inclusion of many whole berries results in a very gradual, gentle extraction as the berries squash over five to seven days in the main period of fermentation. Introducing a gentle foot mixing at about 4 to 5 Baume (two-thirds of the way through fermentation) works to cool the skins and to avoid the broader, oilier, fatter, shorter palate as well as clumsy, quick-ageing tannins (produced by alcohol and heat), and also to increase extraction, particularly mineral extraction.

In addition to the stainless steel fermenters, we felt that existing designs were limiting so we designed and built our own. The gentleness of basket pressing is advantageous in producing fine wine. Unlike many of the alternatives, there are no sharp edges that extract harsh tannins. The basket press allows small parcels to be kept separate. It is also much quicker to complete a cycle, which is particularly important when doing whites. When pressing white varieties we use a pallet plastic bag over the cages to ensure an environment of CO_2. The presses filter out unwanted solids, allowing for full solids ferments with whites or leaving on lees in barrel.

Leaving on the lees (solids) in barrel is a good way of reducing oxidation, and because our methods are so gentle the lees are largely pulp and yeast. The layer that settles in the barrel is quite thin and therefore doesn't putrefy as thick solids can; lees are reductive and are balanced out by the oxidative effect of wooden barrels. It also layers the oak and reduces its influence on the finished wine. This produces a wine that is fresher, fruitier and free of obvious oak.

These processes mean much less racking is required, reducing costs and negative impacts on the wine, but also keep barrels separate, maximising the quality by reducing cross-infection of barrels within a group of one fermenter. The baskets are now made of stainless steel, which means they are stronger and the gaps more consistent and more sterile than the traditional wood baskets. The bottom half of the cages are tapered slightly outwards, eliminating the need to undo them. The baskets are removed and emptied with a forklift, which increases efficiency and reduces the risk of injury.

Observations from winemaking and wine drinking

To be or not to be fault-free

For me, winemaking is the caressing of grapes into wine, but it is also the manipulation of winemaker-induced faults.

All wine has varied amounts of nearly all the faults that exist in wine. Small amounts of faults are not really faults at all but rather part of the complexities of wine, adding and sometimes promoting flavour and interest.

Wine can be grouped into two categories:

- Wines that are designed to be consumed young. These wines can be very flavoursome and complex but will not develop with age.
- Wines that age. In my opinion, great wine can be measured in two ways: by its quality alone, or by the fact that it ages a long time, developing a great life balance and fruit when very old.

Of course many wines fall in between and much commercial wine is just quaffable. These notes, however, are more concerned with the making of *great wine*.

Hydrogen sulphide and reduced characters

Some would argue that any reduced characters are a negative, masking the fruit character and adding characters such as cheesiness, rotten egg gas and grubbiness. However, history shows us reduced characters can help stave off oxidation. Prior to the millennium a common rule of thumb for picking French white wine was: if it showed cheesiness it was probably French. It had an interesting preserving affect. Wines sealed with corks age at different rates depending on the amount of oxygen each cork lets in. A wine showing lots of reduced character sealed with a very good cork or screw cap through which no oxygen permeates will take a long time to lose its reduced character. If the wine has the right make-up it may look amazing when very old. If that wine was cleaned up with copper before bottling, oxidation reactions will occur faster, without the preserving effect of the reduction. Not all wines have the right make-up for ageing; some may just go grubbier as more complex characters are produced and the fruit just falls away. However, the wine produced in many great vineyards can age for an enormously long time, especially with the right amount and type of reduced character.

Over the past decade many producers have chosen to remove any reduced characters completely. This, combined with the reduction in the quality of corks, has tended to produce a much shorter ageing wine, especially if a poor cork allows oxygen to leak through.

At d'Arenberg I choose to keep a small amount of reduced characters in the

wines so as to produce more ageworthy wines. When it comes to red wines I haven't used copper for many years, opting for aeration of only the most overtly reduced wines (less than 1 per cent of a vintage). This also helps to produce an ageworthy wine as copper is a catalyst to oxidation (that is, it speeds it up).

Sulphur dioxide

Sulphur dioxide (SO_2) is used as a preservative in wine to reduce the speed of oxidation. If used in excess, the effect can cause a pricking in the nose or provoke a cough sensation in the throat during the aftertaste of a wine. It is often visible in recently bottled white wines but very, very rarely in reds, as the SO_2 is quickly bound. To produce the most ageworthy wine, SO_2 should be present in abundance. As molecular SO_2 (the part that affects the olfactory system the most) disappears with time, the amount required in the wine depends almost totally on when the wine will be released/consumed. It is necessary to bottle the wine with high SO_2 if it is to be released years down the track.

To fine or not to fine (polyphenols/tannins)

Fining of wines to reduce aggressive harsh characters is a very common practice in winemaking. The unsavoury characters can take the form of course bitterness, hard green characters or excessive tannins, which can be fine and powdery right through to big and chunky.

The perfect wine, in my opinion, is one that needs no fining and ages forever. To achieve a wine like this requires great grapes that have right type of polyphenols (tannins) and are free of polyphenol oxidase enzymes. Grapes that are shrivelled or grown in hotter environments may have considerable amounts of fast-ageing tannins only good for making early drinking wines. The extraction temperatures will also have an impact on the type, amounts and ageworthiness of the tannins (a huge area that will not be covered here).

The skins of the grape then ideally need to be extracted using solvents rather than mechanical means to acquire the correct tannins and flavours. The correct tannins do have an antioxidant effect; however, the higher the volume, the longer they take to polymerise and soften, and they may last longer than the fruit does.

The fashion now is not to fine wine at all. Fining, in this case, involves removing some polyphenols by the addition of a protein (that is, gelatine, milk, egg, fish bladder or, at one time, blood, although this last additive is no longer used or indeed legal).

Every ferment is tasted and pressed off the skins when the right amounts of tannins have been extracted to balance the wine. If the tannins are very mineral orientated, the acidity, tannin and fruit characters are tasted at once. High minerality and lower other tannins is the mecca of wines. In my opinion, these mineral tannins age the slowest and, as they soften over time, open to yield more fruit character that had been concealed tightly in the tannin.

Fining wine to reduce tannins is a tricky exercise, as it often removes as much or more minerality than the unattractive tannins it is aimed at. I see this often in the form of a last-minute fining to make the wine not quite as raw. Unfortunately, it has just removed a bunch of the ageing potential. I believe there is some justification for fining to remove polyphenol oxidose or polyphenols with fast-ageing potential enzymes only if they are present.

Wine style/alcohol/residual sugar/oak

Up to the 1980s most people picked the grapes for dry reds between 12 and 13 Baume. My magical figure was 12.7 Baume so as to produce a more elegant wine. This is strange to talk about now, as reds coming in at this Baume would be considered less than in their prime. Interestingly, Johnny Glatzer of Wolf Blass has used the same figure. Some winemakers have even gone as low as 10.5 Baume for Cabernet Sauvignon, claiming great varietal character and a very leafy characteristic was evident in the final wine. One winemaker with whom I chatted said, 'Amazing it is that this new wine in 20 years will hardly change'. I pointed out that we don't like the character now and I can't see why we would like it in 20 years' time!

In the mid 1980s I picked some reds at 13.5 to 14.5 Baume and had old winemakers from McLaren Vale asking me, 'What characters and flavours are you getting there?' Part of the reason these higher sugars were achieved is the long lead time of getting a harvester in to pick the grapes. At these higher sugar levels bigger, richer wines were achieved. In the 1990s this riper trend took hold, entrenching itself into most Australian reds, and this was particularly brought on by some trendsetting, influential journalists at the time. It became quite a game to see how far the alcohol and fatness of the wine could be pushed. Many winemakers found they could add copious amounts of toasty oak, which would enrich the wine even more. Picking at enormous sugar levels became common for some winemakers, who achieved over 16 per cent alc./vol. This often resulted in wines that had not finished fermentation and retained 8–12 g/l of sugar. Not a problem as far as the winemaker felt; it made an even richer wine. Suddenly by the new millennium we have a style of wine that resembles nothing from the past. Even great vintage port material was not picked excessively ripe in the 1980s or earlier (often only 14–15 Baume).

With Australia's amazing export boom through the 1990s and 2000s, many countries thought there must be something to the idea and have followed this lead to a degree; however, very few examples have pushed so far as the Australian version. These young, very ripe, enormously rich wines are quite a bit of fun, still offering some floweriness. However, they age quickly and after a few years are more reminiscent of partly rectified sump oil that is syrupy with harsh, dead, very dry tannins followed by a hot alcoholic burn. Many of these wines sell for huge dollars to unsuspecting connoisseurs. It is true that many modern drinkers do not age wines and are quite comfortable drinking this style; however, traditional consumers of fine, ageworthy wines have been disgusted to taste these abominations after forking out so much money and leaving them in the cellar for years.

There is no doubt that picking very ripe grapes will make a wine with less ageing potential, and as great wine must age well (by my definition) the pursuit of these styles will not aid a winery's reputation in the long run. At d'Arenberg I never went down this extreme route and over recent years have pulled back the ripeness and oak level even more. I have avoided the road of residual sugar (RS) in red wines.

White wines over the past decade in Australia have also been pared back, with less oak, less malo and finer, longer ageing styles, which is all good as far as I'm concerned. Also in the past decade more Rieslings with residual sugar are popping up. At d'Arenberg we have worked very hard to find the best sites for Riesling in McLaren Vale and have pruned back vines to achieve consistent, just ripe grapes with high acidity, minerals and sherbet characters. This style can comfortably be drunk only with RS of up to 15 g/l.

Currently there are many opinions regarding spontaneous natural fermentation. Much texture can be gained by letting the natural flora (NF) ferment the juice. However, I have opted for partial blending with NF as some fragrance, elegance and fine length is lost.

Many great winemakers have described great wines as being nervous wines that are tense and closed when young. Modern consumers and journalists often don't make allowances for this ageing phase and ridicule the wine before it has had time to develop. Many great, very ageable vintages have passed, swept under the carpet, only to evolve into great old wines with plenty more ageworthiness. The obsession to 'point' wines has unfortunately had its casualties and is part of the reason many wines are being produced in a more forward, less tight style. Add to this the advent of mechanical micro-oxygenation and concentrating techniques, and the results are wines with more sameness and less *terroir*, and often more open wines. Time will show how far Australia can go with these techniques and whether they are allocated to commercial wines only. At d'Arenberg we don't use micro-oxygenation or practise any wine concentration.

Organics/biodynamics

Organics and biodynamics have become very trendy now. With minimal input viticulture practices we are one step away from organic. Some growers who have opted for biodynamic growing have used large amounts of fertiliser, resulting in inferior grapes. In our trials at d'Arenberg, by using a low nitrogen version of biodynamics, we have produced wines with more evident texture but less floral character and length. However, this trial is only three years old and more trialling is required.

pH/acidity

With the right mix of slow-ageing polyphenols and in absence of polyphenol oxyidase enzymes, the pH of wine can be raised. All being equal, higher pH wines will age faster as reactions speed up with the rise in pH. Also, at higher pH levels wines become much more vulnerable to spoilage by bacteria and yeast (for example, Brettanomyces). Bret exists in all wines, but once over the olfactory threshold it has a major negative effect on the wine.

In McLaren Vale and Adelaide Hills the grapes are blessed with good to very good acidity levels and in many years have not required adjustment. At d'Arenberg, we work on keeping the reds under 3.6 pH as over 3.65 pH every prescription of tartrates will increase the pH while under this the pH will go down. This avoids the problems of higher acids combined with high pH. However, the most important thing with all wines is that the acidity is appropriate for the wine and that it is integrated and balanced.

Districts of McLaren Vale

A life spent living and working in McLaren Vale, together with a naturally curious mind, has helped Chester gain a wealth of knowledge about the region. As well as extensive vineyard holdings, d'Arenberg sources grapes from more than 120 growers (depending on the year) who follow the same minimal input philosophies discussed above. These vineyards stretch the length and breadth of the region and grow over 30 grape varieties. This spread of vineyards, along with the combination of growing methods and small-batch winemaking techniques, has allowed Chester to develop an intimate understanding of McLaren Vale.

It's a region that requires careful study, with a number of variable factors that have a strong influence on the wines. These factors include ocean breezes, a big altitude variance from the low-lying beachside vineyards to Blewitt Springs in the foothills of the Mount Lofty Ranges, undulating terrain, and a plethora of soil and geology types. It is this final influence that has been the focus of recent study and has provided another layer of understanding for local winemakers. In this final section Chester explains how these differences translate into unique characters in wine. He also gives some analysis of the temperature variances between the districts.

The production of a geology map in 2010 has given new impetus to the task of redefining the districts of McLaren Vale. A rough map loosely based on soils and distance from the sea was produced in the 1980s, when a vineyard benchmarking exercise was established. Before long this became the map of the districts of McLaren Vale. It probably should never have been used as such, and other than Blewitt Springs very few districts appeared on labels. In 2010 a committee was formed to identify districts with individual wine characters. At the time of writing it has been proposed that the area be divided into 19 districts, with the names still under discussion.

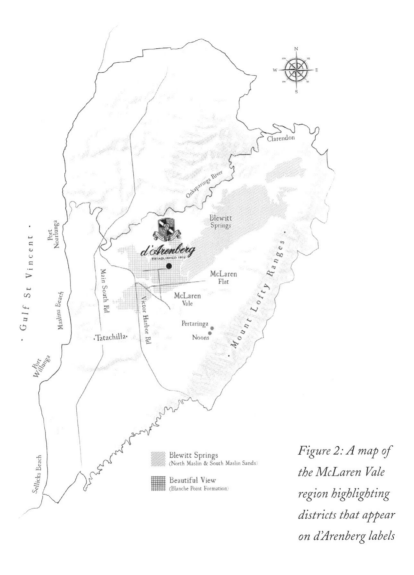

Figure 2: A map of
the McLaren Vale
region highlighting
districts that appear
on d'Arenberg labels

193

On the map in figure 2, we have introduced two likely districts that already appear on the d'Arenberg labels. Rather than listing the distinctions of each individual district, I will describe the variations in a general way with regard to red wines.

The most recently planted part of McLaren Vale is that near Sellicks Beach. The wines from here are more juicy with less fragrant length, sometimes with reasonably blocky tannins. As we move north-east along the young alluvial geological formation to Pertaringa and Noons, the wines gradually lift in floweriness and fragrant length as altitude and proximity to the ocean increase. These wines still retain the juicy characters.

A notable difference is detected when moving just inland of Maslins Beach, where more rich tannins and more soil characters are found in the wine. Moving eastwards again, fragrance rises with the increase in altitude and also because of the sand dunes of the Piramimma Sandstone. Often seen as sand over clay, these formations further increase fragrance because of the sandy soil surface (which allows more moisture in), and the clay underneath maintains good palate weight as well. The liveliness of these wines is greater than of the wines to the south. The more inland we move, the more fragrant and elegant the wines become. The alluvial flats around here are highly variable, often able to produce high yields and more dilute wines if pushed with fertiliser and water.

To the north and north-west of the McLaren Vale township we find the majority of the Blanche Point formation in the district called Beautiful View. The geology here has lots of calcareous material. The wines from this area have substantial amounts of minerality, with some showing considerable gutsiness, fragrance, length and varietal character. Pockets of Piramimma Sandstone can also be found that again give more fragrance and elegance to the wines. More pockets can be found further to the north, although the sand is often blown off and the wines show considerable tannins. Surrounding these pockets are some very old geological formations with less mineral availability. It can be difficult to get commercial yields from these without fertiliser. Pronounced tannins and a good strength of varietal character can be seen in these wines. Sometimes the minerality is overpowered by the blocky tannins, especially in hot years.

To the east we find the large district of Blewitt Springs. Here the geology is mainly Maslin sands. The altitude rises to 200 metres here, which, combined with the more continental positioning and the deep mature sand, is why this part of McLaren Vale produces the most fragrant and elegant wines. Cool, wet years can cause considerable problems in this district, while in hot, dry years it performs well, ripening quite late.

Vineyards further north near Clarendon are also located at high altitude and some distance from the ocean but are on formations that yield more tannins if grown without fertiliser, although this may not be economical. Cooler climate characters also prevail here.

Most of the grapes used for d'Arenberg wine are from the districts of Beautiful View and Blewitt Springs and the Pirramimma Sandstone sand dunes around McLaren Flat. These areas are where most of the older vines are planted and are cooler than the districts to the south. High levels of fragrance and/or minerality are seen in the wines from these districts.

Temperatures of McLaren Vale districts

No registered weather station exists in McLaren Vale except near the coast in Noarlunga, where there are no vines. Six privately owned weather stations in different districts of McLaren Vale have now amassed nine years of data. Figure 3 shows the variation in Mean January Temperatures (MJT) of each district for each year alongside a few other South Australian sites for comparison. The MJT

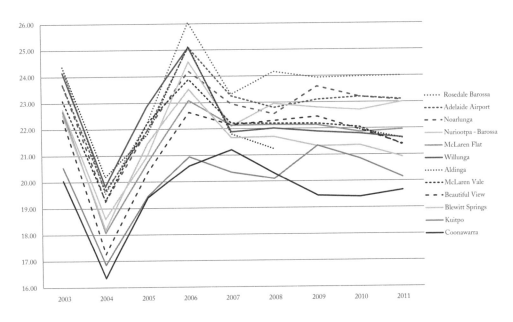

Figure 3: Mean January Temperatures (MJT), McLaren Vale districts, 2003–11

196

may vary not only from year to year (often by as much as 5°C) but also from district to district within a year (up to as much as 2.5°C across the McLaren Vale districts). Using this data and extrapolating the nine years to long-term data (comparing older weather stations nearby with the nine years looked at here), we see in figure 4 that Beautiful View, Blewitt Springs and McLaren Flat are considerably cooler on average than the township of McLaren Vale and points further south. Again, several other regions are included for comparative interest.

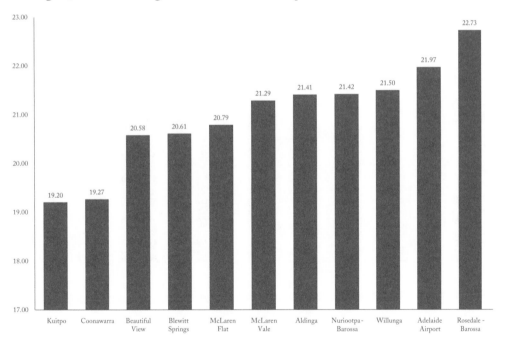

Figure 4: Long-term average MJT, McLaren Vale districts

Heat Degree Days (HDD) is measured by taking the average temperature per day (°C) minus 10 multiplied by the number of days in the seven-month growing season (October to April in the southern hemisphere). The base is 10 because vines do not function below 10°C. Figure 5 shows the HDD for each of the McLaren Vale districts. The same differences can be seen here as in the MJT, although Willunga is considerably warmer. McLaren Vale compares similarly to well-known winemaking regions of Barolo and the southern Rhône.

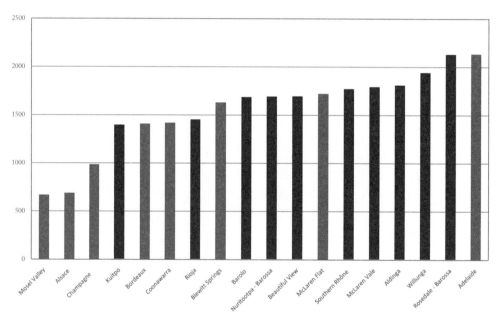

Figure 5: Long-term average HDD, McLaren Vale districts

Endnotes

Introduction

1   Rosemary Burden, *Wines & Wineries of the Southern Vales*, Rigby Limited, 1976, pp. 13–14.

2   ibid., p. 15.

3   H E Laffer, *The Wine Industry of Australia*, Australian Wine Board, Adelaide, 1949, p. 49.

4   Max Lake, *Classic Wines of Australia*, Jacaranda Press, Brisbane, 1966, p. 21.

5   J Robinson, *Oxford Companion to Wine*, Oxford University Press, New York, 2006. Online version <www.jancisrobinson.com/ocw/CH3442.html>.

Chapter 1

1   Rowen Osborn Collection.

2   The Commonwealth Electoral Roll for the Richmond West Polling Place in the Division of Yarra confirms this for the years 1903 and 1905.

3   Details taken from the biographical entry 'Joseph Rowe Osborn, J.P.', published in the *Cyclopedia of South Australia*, 1908, pp. 508–9.

4   *Freelance and LV Gazette*, n.d., n.p. Our thanks to Richmond Football Club historian and MCC Assistant Librarian, Trevor Ruddell, for this information.

5   His membership card and some old account books are held by the family.

6   In 1993 Margaret (Peg) Thornley, Nancy Hayward's sister, related to Rowen Osborn that she had been given a bracelet by Joseph R Osborn's other daughter, Edith, and that it had been won by Joseph on Oaks Day. The bracelet contained a large sapphire, which Peg had had remodelled before giving it to her granddaughter. Joseph Osborn's most significant win on Oaks Day was with Thunder Queen in 1896, but no other record of his prize (including a bracelet) has been found.

7   His name is absent for the years 1896–97 and 1898–99. R F Osborn, *J R Osborn and His Racehorses*, self-published, Canberra, 2001, p. 19.

8   One witness to the marriage was J Stewart, coachbuilder of Winlaton, probably Mary's brother, John.

9   'Joseph Rowe Osborn, J.P.', *Cyclopedia of South Australia*, 1908, pp. 508–9.

10 Edward's death occurred five days after Mary's youngest sister, Florence Frederika Stewart, aged 15, died of the same disease.

11 Bayfield Moulden had convened the meeting out of which the South Australian Football Association grew in 1878. Joseph

and Beaumont served as Town Clerks at Norwood and were partners in a legal practice. Bayfield Moulden built a stone house of eight rooms in 1879–80 on eight acres. In 1881 he sold four acres, which is now 4 Philip Street.

12 Elizabeth Warburton, *The Paddocks Beneath: A History of Burnside from the Beginning*, Corporation of the City of Burnside, South Australia, 1981, p. 64.

13 Subdivision plan no. 566 of 1877 covered 22 acres. Their plan created 94 building allotments and the South Australian Company, in plan 1356 of 1884, created another 104 (presumably on the 67 acres it had not sold in its original 134 acres).

14 Warburton, op. cit., p. 70.

15 Osborn, op. cit., Canberra, 2001.

16 Another investment was in the gold-mining company Wellington Alluvials. When the J R Osborn Family Trusts were wound up in August 1958, 742 shares in Wellington Alluvials were still held. Though they were valued at sixpence each, they were said to have provided a good return in the past.

17 After the sale of James Marshall & Company in 1928, Jim bought a 6000-acre sheep property, 'Mageppa', 40 miles from Naracoorte, South Australia, on the Victorian side of the border. The Marshalls sold 'Darroch' and built a house on 'Mageppa', where they lived until the early 1940s. Jim died in 1946 and Mary in 1970.

18 After a successful career in the wine industry, Sam died on 8 February 1966, aged 73; Edith died in Angaston, near Nuriootpa, on 7 September 1981, aged 90.

19 Frederick Slaney-Poole (1845–1936). Poole and his wife had eight children and he was said to have been a martinet in family life. Their eldest son, Thomas (1873–1923), became a Judge of the Supreme Court of South Australia and was for a time Acting Chief Justice and also Administrator in the absence of the Governor. In 1903 he married Dora Williams in St Peter's College Chapel. Seventeen years later Frank Osborn married Dora Slaney-Poole's niece, Helen d'Arenberg, in the same place. Rowen Osborn draft manuscript.

20 The book was *The Ingoldsby Legends*. Both books remain in the library at McLaren Vale.

21 He passed in English Literature, Latin, French, Arithmetic and Algebra, and Geometry.

22 The *Chronicle* reporter concluded that his presence did not help much: 'Osborn F has made little improvement. His defence is weak but [he] has a punishing offstroke. Slow in the field.' The first half of the 1906 season was a little more successful for Frank; he was fourth in the batting averages and third in bowling with six wickets. The *Chronicle* concluded that he, among others, 'with earnest, steady practice should do well'.

23 *Prince Alfred College Chronicle*, no. 87, January 1907, p. 448.

24 *The Scotch Collegian*, October 1907, vol. IV, no. 3, pp. 109–10.

25 *Prince Alfred College Chronicle*, no. 90, January 1908, p. 580.

26 ibid., p. 589.

27 University were dismissed for 337, Frank

taking 0 for 55 off 13 overs.

28 Adelaide *Advertiser*, 11 March 1911.

29 One record of a cricket match played against Trinity College in March 1911 has been found. The scores were: Ormond 304 and 101 (Osborn 29) and Trinity 474 (Osborn 1 catch). One scorer for Trinity was a freshman from Melbourne Grammar School, Edmund Herring, who later became Lieutenant General Sir Edmund Herring, Lieutenant Governor and Chief Justice.

30 Fay Woodhouse, 'A Place Apart: A Study of Student Political Engagement at the University of Melbourne 1930–1939',

unpublished PhD thesis, Department of History, University of Melbourne, 2001, p. 49.

31 Rosemary Burden, *Wines and Wineries of the Southern Vales*, Rigby, Adelaide, 1975, p. 123.

32 Rowen Osborn, conversation with Mrs Muirhead and Mrs Renfrey, 'The Miltons', draft manuscript.

33 Adelaide *Advertiser*, 25 August 1915.

34 E J Colliver & B H Richardson, *The Forty-third: The Story and Official History of the 43rd Battalion, AIF*, Rigby, Adelaide, 1920, p. 12.

35 ibid., p. 5.

36 ibid., p. 13.

37 ibid.

Chapter 2

1 Geoffrey Haydon Manning, *Hope Farm: Cradle of the McLaren Vale Wine Industry*, Adelaide, 1980, p. 11–12; Mike Potter, *Wines and Wineries of South Australia*, Rigby, Adelaide, 1978, p. 2, 62.

2 Barrans is described on the land grant as a currier of Mitcham, now a suburb of Adelaide.

3 Charles Sturt (1795–1869) was born in Bengal and educated in England at Harrow School. He led two inland expeditions and established the extent and interconnected flows of Australia's inland river systems. In 1939 he was judged by historian Ernest Scott in 1939 to be the 'greatest Australian explorer'. In 1832 he published *Two Expeditions into the Interior of Southern Australia*, which persuaded Wakefield that the country described was ideal for his proposed experiment. *The Wakefield Companion to South*

Australian History, Wakefield Press, Kent Town, 2001, pp. 522–3.

4 The South Australian Death Register states he was born in 1798, although it may have been 1792.

5 In 1853 Barrans was one of about 120 people to sign a petition to the Lieutenant-Governor appealing that the southern portion of the electoral district of West Torrens become the District of Mitcham. The petition was successful.

6 The Torrens System of titles is a statutory system of registration of title, designed to facilitate and simplify the transfer of land. It was named after Sir Robert Torrens (1814–1884). Torrens' Bill was introduced into the Legislative Assembly on 4 June 1857, received assent on 27 January 1858 and came into operation on 1 July 1858. Queensland

adopted the system in 1861; New South Wales, Victoria and Tasmania in 1870; and Western Australia in 1875. A W Jose and W J Carter, *The Australian Encyclopedia*, p. 565.

7   *Winery Buildings in South Australia 1836 to 1936: The Southern Districts*, Architecture Papers, University of Adelaide, n.d., held in Willunga Library.

8   The property remained mortgaged to William Pavy until his death on 13 January 1908, when the mortgage was transferred to Pavy's executors, his brothers Richard Pavy of Crystal Brook and Albert Pavy of Milang. The mortgage was discharged on 1 April 1908.

9   Land Order No. 733, issued in England. The northern three-fifths of Section 128 was bought by the Osborn family from R N Spong on 28 November 1958.

10 Letter from Department of Lands to Rowen Osborn, 22 April 1988.

11 The house, with its rooms built side by side, is described by the writer as 'like a railway carriage'. E H Hallack, *Our Townships, Farms and Households — Southern Districts of South Australia*, Adelaide, 1892.

12 Young had the land brought under the Real Property Act and a Certificate of Title was issued in his name on 27 October 1870.

13 Adolphus William Young was born at Hare Hatch House, Berkshire, England, in 1814. He married in 1837 and migrated to Australia, arriving in Sydney where he became a provisional director of the Australian Gaslight Company, third police magistrate and a Justice of the Peace. In March 1838 he resigned his magistracy, regarding the salary of £300 as inadequate, and joined the legal firm of Carr and Rogers as an attorney. Late in 1839 he was involved in a dispute with the Australian Gaslight Company and found guilty 'of indiscretion'. In 1840 he returned to England. However, he returned to Australia in October 1842 and took up the position of sheriff of New South Wales on 2 July 1843. His first wife died in 1847 and he married Jane Throsby, eldest daughter of Charles Throsby of Throsby Park, near Berrima, in New South Wales. He resigned from the position in November 1849 and with Jane and his children returned to England where he lived at Hare Hatch House, which he had inherited from his father. He represented Great Yarmouth (a Norfolk seat) in the House of Commons in 1857–59 and Helston (Cornwall) from 1868 to 1879. In Parliament he showed a keen interest in Australian affairs. Young's second wife also predeceased him and he married a third time. He died at Hare Hatch House on 4 November 1885, leaving an estate of some £27 000 to his widow and eight surviving children. A F Pike, 'Young, Adolphus William (1814–1885)', *Australian Dictionary of Biography*, vol. 2, Melbourne University Press, 1967, pp. 633–4.

14 Manning, op. cit.

15 Rowen Osborn, conversation with Mrs Verna Jacobs, 1989, 'The Miltons', Rowen Osborn draft manuscript.

16 James Halliday, *Varietal Wines*, HarperCollins, Sydney, 2004, p. 202. Halliday here quotes Sir John Macarthur, an early participant in the Australian

wine industry.

17 ibid., p. 244.

18 Barbara Santich, *McLaren Vale Sea and Vines*, Wakefield Press, Kent Town, 1998, p. 54.

19 Halliday, *Varietal Wines*, p. 203.

20 ibid., p. 203.

21 'The South Australian Position', *Wine and Spirit News and Australian Vigneron*, 25 February 1916, p. 51.

22 ibid., p. 51.

23 Halliday, *Varietal Wines*, op. cit. p. 226.

24 H E Laffer, *The Wine Industry of Australia*, Australian Wine Board, Adelaide 1949, p. 125.

25 This tank was finally cut up in 1954 and the iron flattened and used for a grape tray on a trolley, and in 1955 to extend the motor shed. Rowen Osborn draft manuscript.

26 'The S.A. viticultural industry: more optimistic winemen', *Australian Brewing and Wine Journal*, 20 August 1921, p. 692.

27 ibid.

28 Walter Phillips, ' "Six o'clock swill": the introduction of early closing of hotel bars in Australia', *Historical Studies*, vol. 19, no. 75, October 1980, pp. 250–66.

29 'Soldier Vignerons: Advice from the South Australian Alliance', *The Australian Brewing and Wine Journal*, 20 August 1921, p. 682.

30 ibid.

31 'Adelaide Notes', *Wine and Spirit News and Australian Vigneron*, 30 June 1928, p. 312.

32 Laffer, op. cit., p. 125.

33 Rosemary Burden, *Wines and Wineries of the Southern Vales*, Rigby, Adelaide, 1975, p. 123.

34 John Beeston, *A Concise History of Australian Wine*, Allen & Unwin, St Leonards, 2005, p. 155.

35 'Wonderful progress of the wine industry in Australia', *Wine and Spirit News and Australian Vigneron*, 30 April 1928, p. 221.

36 'Adelaide Notes', *Wine and Spirit News and Australian Vigneron*, 30 June 1928, p. 312.

37 *Wine and Spirit News and Australian Vigneron*, 30 September 1928, p. 461.

38 Burden, op. cit.

39 Peter Bond Burgoyne had established a business in London importing Australian wines in the 1880s.

40 O L Zeigler, 'Francis Ernest Osborn, "Bundarra" Vineyards', *Vines and Vineyards of South Australia*, Mail Newspaper Pty Ltd, Adelaide, 1928, pp. 256–7.

41 ibid., p. 257.

Chapter 3

1 Adelaide *Advertiser*, 27 September 1895, n.p.

2 Frederick and Albert Kay were local winemakers and kept diaries from 1879 to the 1960s.

3 Wednesday 18 November 1896, Kay Diaries. In possession of Mr Colin Kay, Kay Brothers Pty Ltd, McLaren Vale.

4 Adelaide *Advertiser*, 27 June 1908, p. 10.

5 Adelaide *Advertiser*, 3 February 1913. In the section 'Less than five subjects' passed, Helen's name is included. The other subjects for examination included English History,

Geography, Greek, Latin, French, German, Arithmetic, Algebra, Geometry, Physics, Inorganic Chemistry, Psychology and Botany.

6 'Patriotic Bridge', *The Mail*, 27 May 1916, p. 12.

7 Adelaide *Mail*, 3 June 1916, p. 8, and 3 June 1916, p. 5.

8 Conversation between Rowen Osborn and Elizabeth Auld, 1993.

9 A.M.U.A. denotes Associate of Music University of Adelaide.

10 'Queen's Hall', *The Register*, Adelaide, 14 November 1917, p. 8.

11 Trinity College of Music, London, then conferred (as it still does) Associate (ATCL), Licentiate (LTCL) and Fellowship (FTCL) diplomas in music performance. In 2005 Trinity College of Music and Laban, a leading centre of music and contemporary dance, came together to form Trinity Laban Conservatoire of Music and Dance.

12 Helen travelled on the Blue Funnel liner the *Ascanius*. Reports of the passenger list appeared in both the *Register* and the *Advertiser*, 16 May 1919, p. 8.

13 Letter from Frank Osborn to Rowen Osborn, 9 February 1957. Letter in possession of Rowen Osborn, Canberra.

14 The garage was always referred to as the 'motor shed'.

15 'McLaren Vale Southern Districts War Memorial Hospital Appeal', Adelaide *Advertiser*, 11 December 1947, p. 5.

16 'About People by Lady Kitty', Adelaide *Advertiser*, 11 October 1945, p. 3.

17 'About People by Lady Kitty', Adelaide *Advertiser*, 29 November 1945, p. 3.

18 John Beeston, *A Concise History of Australian Wine*, Allen & Unwin, St Leonards, 2005, pp. 181–200.

19 'Girls Shown Over Carrier', Adelaide *Mail*, 29 June 1946, p. 2.

20 'About People by Lady Kitty', 20 February 1948, p. 5; 'Women's Bowls Results', 21 February 1948, p. 5; 'Farewell Party at Berkley', Adelaide *Advertiser*, 25 February 1948, p. 5.

21 'Cabaret Dance', Adelaide *Mail*, 14 September 1946, p. 8.

22 'UK Jobs "Easy" for Australian Typists', Adelaide *Advertiser*, 7 June 1950, p. 11.

23 For example, in September 1946, when a third-year student, Jeanie Susman, gave a buffet dinner before going to the science dance at the Refectory, Rowen was among her guests. This social snippet made it into the pages of the Adelaide *Mail*, 14 September 1946, p. 9.

24 'University College Commencement', *Canberra Times*, 29 March 1950, p. 4; 'UK Jobs "Easy" for Australian Typists', op. cit.; 'Bachelors...' The *Mail*, 7 October 1950, p. 40.

25 'The Younger Set', Adelaide *Advertiser*, 4 November 1952, p. 6.

26 Susan Marsden, J D Somerville Oral History Collection, State Library of South Australia: Interview no. OH 768/1, transcript p. 7.

Chapter 4

1   Robert Osmond and Kym Anderson, *Trends and Cycles in the Australian Wine Industry 1850 to 2000*, Centre for International Economic Studies, University of Adelaide, 1998, p. 7.

2   ibid., p. 9.

3   d'Arry's diary, 1950, transcribed by Rowen Osborn, Osborn Collection, McLaren Vale.

4   d'Arry Osborn, interview with Fay Woodhouse, 30 November 2010, transcript p. 1.

5   ibid., p. 1.

6   ibid., p. 2.

7   Susan Marsden, J D Somerville Oral History Collection, State Library of South Australia, Interview No. OH 768/1, transcript p. 8.

8   d'Arry Osborn, interview with Fay Woodhouse, 30 November 2010, transcript p. 3.

9   ibid., p. 4.

10 ibid., p. 5.

11 ibid., p. 5.

12 Elizabeth Warburton, *The Paddocks Beneath: A History of Burnside from the Beginning*, the Corporation of the City of Burnside, South Australia, 1981, p. 64.

13 John Beeston, *A Concise History of Australian Wine*, Allen & Unwin, St Leonards, 2005, p. 181; H E Laffer, *The Wine Industry of Australia*, Australian Wine Board, Adelaide, 1949, p. 134.

14 James Halliday, *A History of the Australian Wine Industry 1949–1994*, Australian Wine and Brandy Corporation, Adelaide, 1994, p. 3.

15 Osmond and Anderson, op. cit., p. 10.

16 d'Arry Osborn, interview with Fay Woodhouse, 30 November, 2010, transcript p. 14.

17 d'Arry's diary, 1950, Osborn Collection, McLaren Vale.

18 ibid.

19 d'Arry's diary, 1955, Osborn Collection, McLaren Vale.

20 d'Arry's diary, 1956, Osborn Collection, McLaren Vale.

21 Letter from d'Arry Osborn to Rowen Osborn, 19 November 1956, Osborn Collection, McLaren Vale.

22 Graeme Davison, 'Olympic Games', in Andrew Brown-May and Shurlee Swain (eds), *The Encyclopedia of Melbourne*, Cambridge University Press, Melbourne, 2005, pp. 518–19.

23 Walter Phillips, ' "Six o'clock swill": the introduction of early closing of hotel bars in Australia', *Historical Studies,* vol. 19, no. 75, October 1980, pp. 250–66.

24 Nicholas Faith, *Australia's Liquid Gold*, Mitchell Beazley, London, 2002, p. 145.

25 ibid.

26 Anthony Madigan, 'Regional heroes: an hour with the Osborns', *WBM: Australia's Wine Business Magazine*, June 2009, p. 19.

27 d'Arry's diary, 1957, Osborn Collection, McLaren Vale.

28 Obituaries, Mr F E Osborn, *Australian Brewing and Wine Journal*, 21 October 1957, p. 68.

29 ibid.

30 Halliday, *A History of the Australian Wine Industry 1949–1994*, op. cit., p. 5.

31 ibid., p. 14.

32 ibid., p. 15.

33 See Beeston, *Concise History of Australian Wine*, op. cit., pp. 191–2; David Dunstan, 'A Drink Whose Time Had Finally Come: Wine Consumption in Australia 1950–1980' in Robert Crawford, Judith Smart & Kim Humphreys (eds), *Consumer Australia:* *Historical Perspectives*, Cambridge Scholars Publishing, Newcastle, 2010, p. 147; Halliday, *A History of the Australian Wine Industry 1949–1994*, p. 6; Charles Gent, *Mixed Dozen: The Story of Australian Winemaking Since 1788*, Duffy & Snellgrove, Sydney, 2003, pp. 222–3.

Chapter 5

1 d'Arry Osborn, interview with Fay Woodhouse, 30 November 2010, transcript p. 17.

2 James Halliday, *A History of the Australian Wine Industry 1949–1994*, Australian Wine and Brandy Corporation, Adelaide, 1994, p. 6.

3 d'Arry Osborn, interview with Fay Woodhouse, 30 November 2010, transcript p. 17.

4 John Beeston, *A Concise History of Australian Wine*, Allen & Unwin, St Leonards, 2005, pp. 189–91.

5 ibid., p 182.

6 ibid., p. 191.

7 ibid., pp. 190–1.

8 David Dunstan, 'The Wine Press', Food and Drink, *Meanjin*, Vol. 4, 2002, p. 35.

9 Beeston, op. cit., p. 191.

10 d'Arry's diary, 1957, Osborn Collection, McLaren Vale.

11 Letter from d'Arry to Rowen Osborn, 30 October 1957, Osborn Collection, McLaren Vale.

12 Letter from d'Arry to Rowen Osborn, 2 May 1958, Osborn Collection, McLaren Vale.

13 Note here that these measurements are alcohol strength in proof, as opposed to by volume, as we use today. Halliday, *A History of the Australian Wine Industry 1949–1994*, op. cit., p. 20.

14 Letter from d'Arry to Rowen Osborn, 29 May 1958, Osborn Collection, McLaren Vale.

15 *Australian Brewing and Wine Journal*, 20 August 1959, p. 34.

16 *Australian Brewing and Wine Journal*, 21 September 1959, p. 32.

17 d'Arry Osborn, interview with Fay Woodhouse, 30 November 2010, transcript p. 17.

18 City of Onkaparinga Oral History Program in collaboration with State Library of South Australia; interview with d'Arry Osborn at d'Arenberg Winery, McLaren Vale, by Dr Susan Marsden, 16 March 2006, p. 2.

19 Anthony Madigan, '*That* stripe and the old school tie-in', in 'Regional Heroes: An hour with the Osborns', *WBM: Australia's Wine Business Magazine*, June 2009, p. 26.

20 d'Arry Osborn, interview with Fay Woodhouse, 30 November 2010, transcript p. 17.

21 Nicholas Faith, *Liquid Gold: The Story of Australian Wine and its Makers*, Pan MacMillan Australia, Sydney, 2002, p. 183.

22 *Australian Wine, Brewing and Spirit Review*, 21 August 1961, p. 40.

23 *Australian Wine, Brewing and Spirit Review*,

20 March 1963, p. 40.

24 The volume *Planches de l'Armorial général de J.-B. Rietstap*, par V. Rolland, Paris: Institut Héraldique, 1903–1926, is still available at the South Australian State Library and is believed to be the text consulted by d'Arry and Don in 1959.

25 Graeme Lofts, *Heart & Soul: Australia's First Families of Wine*, John Wiley & Sons, Milton, 2010, p. 208.

26 Letter from d'Arry to Rowen Osborn, 12 November 1960, Osborn Collection, McLaren Vale. d'Arry sent samples of his latest wine labels to Rowen.

27 Anthony Madigan, 'Regional heroes — father and son', in *WBM: Australia's Wine Business Magazine*, p. 22.

28 Timeline, d'Arenberg Records and Archives.

29 Faith, op. cit., p. 184.

30 d'Arry's diaries, 1961 and 1962, Osborn Collection, McLaren Vale.

31 Letter from d'Arry to Rowen Osborn, 2 October 1962, Osborn Collection, McLaren Vale.

32 ibid.

33 The 1962 Report of the Australian Wine Board, quoted in Halliday, *A History of the Australian Wine Industry 1949–1994*, p. 22.

34 Beeston, op. cit., p. 205.

35 'Wine firms merge', *The Southern Times*, 15 November 1962.

36 d'Arry's diary and letters, 1963, Osborn Collection, McLaren Vale.

37 *Australian Wine, Brewing and Spirit Review*, 20 August 1962, p. 38.

38 Faith, op. cit., p. 139.

39 David Dunstan, 'Watson, James Calexte (1903–1962)', *Australian Dictionary of Biography*, vol. 16, Melbourne University Press, 2002, pp. 502–3.

40 *Australian Wine, Brewing and Spirit Review*, 20 September 1962, p. 244.

41 Max Lake, quoted in Dunstan, 'A sobering experience: from "Australian Burgundy" to "Kanga Rouge": Australian wine battles on the London market 1900 to 1981', in *Journal of Australian Studies*, vol. 17, no. 2, Winter 2002 (pub. 2004), p. 7.

42 Charles Gent, *Mixed Dozen: The Story of Australian Winemaking Since 1788*, Duffy & Snellgrove, Sydney, 2003, p. 211.

43 Dunstan, 'Words on Wine', op.cit., p. 2.

44 Gent, op. cit., p. 217.

45 d'Arry's diary and letters, 1964, Osborn Collection, McLaren Vale.

46 d'Arry's diary, 1964, Osborn Collection, McLaren Vale.

47 Halliday, *A History of the Australian Wine Industry 1949–1994*, op. cit., p. 6.

48 d'Arry Osborn, interview with Fay Woodhouse, 1 September 2011.

49 Rowen Frederick Osborn, brief curriculum vitae, in possession of Rowen Osborn.

50 Letter from d'Arry to Rowen Osborn, 28 November 1966, Osborn Collection, McLaren Vale.

51 d'Arry's diary, 1967, Osborn Collection, McLaren Vale.

52 Letter from Len Evans to d'Arry Osborn, 4 November 1974, p. 2, Osborn Collection, McLaren Vale.

53 Letter from Research Librarian Trinity

College, Dublin, to Rowen Osborn, 28 October 1974, Rowen Osborn Collection, Canberra.

54 ibid.

55 Law Society of South Australia Index Cards.

56 Trinity College, Dublin, enrolment records. Letter from Research Librarian, Trinity College, Dublin, to Rowen Osborn, 28 October 1974, Rowen Osborn Collection, Canberra.

57 Letter from Research Librarian, Trinity College, Dublin, to Rowen Osborn, 28 October 1974, Rowen Osborn Collection, Canberra.

58 Adelaide *Advertiser*, 2 December 1898, p. 6.

59 He died of tuberculosis on 13 July 1886.

60 David Kelly, *The Ruling Few, or, The Human Background to Diplomacy*, Hollis & Carter, London, 1952, p. 20.

61 ibid.

62 ibid., pp. 20–1.

63 Marriage certificate, 19 December 1894, Rowen Osborn Collection, Canberra.

64 Rowen later sourced an article published in 1974 in the English *Women's Weekly* that featured Prince Arman d'Arenberg, his wife and their home. Rowen Osborn Collection, Canberra.

65 2 August 1974, Francis d'Arenberg Osborn to Prince Erik d'Arenberg, Uruguay, South America. Osborn Correspondence file, d'Arenberg Archives, McLaren Vale.

66 20 January 1975, Duke d'Arenberg to Mrs Antoinette Bourne, Lady M N Kelly and Sir Francis Osborn, pp. 3–4. Osborn Correspondence file, d'Arenberg Archives, McLaren Vale.

67 20 January 1975, Duke d'Arenberg to Mrs Antoinette Bourne, Lady M N Kelly and Sir Francis Osborn, ibid.

68 Memorandum of Advice, F E Osborn & Sons Pty Ltd and d'Arenberg Wines Pty Ltd re Duke d'Arenberg, Use of name d'Arenberg and d'Arenberg Coat of Arms on Wine Labels, June 1975, p. 7. d'Arenberg Archives, McLaren Vale.

69 Undated draft letter to Duke d'Arenberg. Osborn Correspondence file, d'Arenberg Archives, McLaren Vale.

70 d'Arry Osborn, interview with Fay Woodhouse, 30 November 2010, transcript p. 18.

71 9 January [no year], Prince Leopold d'Arenberg, Lausanne, to d'Arry Osborn. d'Arenberg Archives, McLaren Vale.

72 Oral History interview with Dr Susan Marsden, op. cit., transcript p. 5.

73 Obituary, Mr F E Osborn, *Australian Brewing and Wine Journal*, 21 October 1957, p. 68.

Chapter 6

1 From 'Regional heroes', *WBM: Australia's Wine Business Magazine*, June 2009, p. 23.

2 ibid., p. 23.

3 Chester was so named by Australian *Gourmet Traveller Magazine* in an article 'Chester Osborn d'Arenberg', July 2008, p. 45.

4 Chester Osborn, interview with Fay Woodhouse, 1 September 2011.

5   Andrew Jefford, 'The court of Chester', *Waitrose Food Illustrated*, UK, October 2009, p. 88.

6   Andrew Caillard, 'Chester Osborn d'Arenberg', *Gourmet Traveller Magazine*, July 2008, p. 45.

7   ibid.

8   Anthony Madigan, 'Regional heroes: an hour with the Osborns', *WBM: Australia's Wine Business Magazine*, June 2009, p. 19.

9   Caillard, op. cit.

10 Madigan, op. cit., p. 22.

11 'Profile: Succession', in *Winestate*, November/December 1988, p. 38.

12 Caillard, op. cit.

13 Madigan, op. cit., p. 22.

14 Jefford, op. cit., p. 88.

15 Caillard, op. cit.

16 The larger pieces were cleared from the vineyards in the late 1880s and utilised in many of the buildings at d'Arenberg, most notably the old stables.

17 Profile: 'Succession', in *Winestate*, November/December 1988, p. 38.

18 ibid.

19 Caillard, op. cit.

20 Madigan, op. cit., p. 23.

21 Chester Osborn, interview with Fay Woodhouse, 1 September 2011.

22 James Halliday, *A History of the Australian Wine Industry 1949–1994*, Australian Wine and Brandy Corporation, Adelaide, 1994, p. 49.

23 ibid, p. 45.

24 Table 14, 'Volume and unit value...', in Robert Osmond and Kym Anderson, *Trends and Cycles in the Australian Wine Industry 1850 to 2000*, University of Adelaide, 1998, p. 85.

25 Halliday, op. cit., p. 58.

26 James Halliday, *The Australian Wine Compendium*, Angus & Robertson, North Ryde, 1985, p. 449.

27 Robin Bradley, *The Small Wineries of Australia*, Macmillan, South Melbourne, 1986, p. 51.

28 James Halliday's '100 Best Wines', in *The Australian Magazine*, 14–15 November 1992, p. 27.

29 Ralph Kyte-Powell, 'Tastings', *The Melbourne Weekly*, 1–7 June 1993, p. 21.

30 'The d'Arenberg Story', *Cafe Society*, 1993 p. 234.

31 'Gone are the earthy, leathery odours of the '60s and '70s', *Winewise*, vol. 10, no. 4, October 1994, p. 7.

32 *Winestate*, September/October 1993, p. 17.

33 'Halliday's Choice', The Weekend Review, *Weekend Australian*, 10–11 October 1992, d'Arenberg archive.

34 ibid.

35 Chester Osborn, interview with Fay Woodhouse, 1 September 2011.

36 Max Allen, *The Future Makers: Australian Wines for the 21st Century*, Hardie Grant Books, Melbourne, 2010, p. 22.

37 ibid.

38 John Beeston, *A Concise History of Australian Wine*, Allen & Unwin, St Leonards, 2005, pp. 261–2.

39 Don Hogg, 'Tang of the barn', *Herald Sun*, 9 May 1993; 'Vintage year for winemaker', *Southern Cross*, 15 September 1993, p. 15.

40 Invitation to 'Celebrate a Golden Vintage', d'Arenberg Archives, McLaren Vale.

41 Halliday, *The Australian Wine Compendium*,

op. cit., p. 450; 'Tang of the barn', *Herald Sun*, 9 May 1993.

42 Chester Osborn, interview with Fay Woodhouse, 1 September 2011.

43 ibid.

44 ibid.

45 *Australian Gourmet Traveller*, September 2011, p. 102.

46 'SA Sale Price lifts wine area to top of class', *Australian*, 18 June 1997, p. 19.

47 'd'Arenberg Winery increases its holding', *Argus*, 5 June 1997, p. 13.

48 'Wine maker pays record price for farm', Adelaide *Advertiser*, 8 April 1997, p. 5.

49 Chester Osborn, interview with Fay Woodhouse, 30 November 2010, transcript p. 3.

50 James Halliday, *Varietal Wines*, HarperCollins, Sydney, 2004, pp. 244–5.

51 Chester Osborn, interview with Fay Woodhouse, 30 November 2010, transcript p. 2.

52 ibid.

53 d'Arry Osborn, Oral History Interview with Dr Susan Marsden, transcript p. 46.

54 Chester Osborn, interview with Fay Woodhouse, 1 September 2011.

55 Madigan, op. cit., p. 22.

56 d'Arry Osborn, interview with Fay Woodhouse, 30 November 2010, transcript p. 17.

57 Robert Hill Smith, quoted in Max Allen, op. cit., p. 51.

58 Chester Osborn, interview with Fay Woodhouse, 1 September 2011.

59 'Closure Positioning Statement', d'Arenberg Wines, 2005.

60 Chester Osborn, interview with Fay Woodhouse, 1 September 2011.

61 Caillard, op. cit., p. 45.

Notes from the winemaker

The following two notes relate to the temperature graphs on pp. 196–198.

- Australian Bureau of Meteorology (stations 023034, 023343, 023373, 023885, 026091), <www.bom.gov.au>.
- McLaren Vale Grape Wine and Tourism Cropwatch service.

Long-term average annual HDDs for comparable European winemaking districts:

- G V Jones, M A White, O R Cooper & K Storchmann. 'Climate change and global wine quality', Climatic Change, 73(3), 2005, p. 325.

BIBLIOGRAPHY

Archival collections

Rowen Osborn Collection, Canberra
d'Arry Osborn Collection, McLaren Vale
d'Arenberg Records and Archives, McLaren Vale
University of Melbourne Archives, Student Records
University of Adelaide Archives and Adelaide
    Conservatorium of Music Archives
Prince Alfred College Archives and Image
    Collection

Onkaparinga Library, Local History Collection
National Trust of Australia, Willunga, South
    Australia Branch
Trinity Laban Conservatoire of Music and Dance,
    London
Richmond Football Club Archives
Melbourne Cricket Club Archives
National Archives of Australia, Canberra

Books and book chapters

Allen, Max. *The Future Makers: Australian Wines for the 21st Century*, Hardie Grant Books, Melbourne, 2010.

Beeston, John. *A Concise History of Australian Wine*, Allen & Unwin, St Leonards, 2005.

Bell, George. 'Viticulture and winemaking in early South Australia', in *Vineyard of the Empire*, South Australian Centre for Settlement Studies, Australian Industrial Publishers, Adelaide, 1988.

Benwell, W S. *Coonawarra a Vignoble*, Gollin & Co., South Melbourne, 1973.

Bradley, Robin. *The Small Wineries of Australia: A Guide to the Best Makers*, revised and updated, Macmillan, South Melbourne, 1986.

——. *The Small Wineries of Australia: A Guide to the Best Makers*, Macmillan, South Melbourne, 1982.

——. *Australian Wine Vintages*, 2nd edn, 1981.

——. *The Australian Wine Pocket Book*, Macmillan, South Melbourne, 1979.

Burden, Rosemary. *Wines and Wineries of the Southern Vales*, Rigby, Adelaide, 1975.

H T Burgess, editor. *The Cyclopedia of South Australia in Two Volumes: an Historical and Commercial Review, Descriptive and Biographical Facts, Figures and Illustrations: an Epitome of Progress*, 1907-09

Colliver, E J, & Richardson, B H. *The Forty Third: The Story and Official History of the 43rd Battalion, AIF*, Rigby, Adelaide, 1920.

Cyclopedia of South Australia, Adelaide, 1908.

Davison, Graeme. 'Olympic Games', in Andrew Brown-May & Shurlee Swain (eds), *The Encyclopedia of Melbourne*, Cambridge University Press, Melbourne, 2005.

Dunstan, David. 'A drink whose time had finally come: wine consumption in Australia 1950–1980', in Robert Crawford, Judith Smart & Kim Humphrey (eds), *Consumer Australia: Historical Perspectives*, Cambridge Scholars Publishing,

Newcastle, 2010.

——. 'Watson, James Calexte (1903–1962)', *Australian Dictionary of Biography*, vol. 16, Melbourne University Press, 2002.

Dunstan, David, & Chaitman, Annette. 'Food and drink: the appearance of a publishing subculture', in David Carter & Anne Galligan (eds), *Making Books: Contemporary Australian Publishing*, University of Queensland Press, St Lucia, 2007.

Evans, Len. *Australia and New Zealand Complete Book of Wine*, Hamlyn, Sydney, 1973.

Faith, Nicholas. *Australia's Liquid Gold*, Mitchell Beazley, London, 2002.

Gent, Charles. *Mixed Dozen: The Story of Australian Winemaking since 1788*, Duffy & Snellgrove, Sydney, 2003.

Gregory, J, & Gothard, J. *Historical Encyclopedia of Western Australia*, University of Western Australia Press, 2009.

Hall, Denis, & Hankel, Valmai. *Wine-Growing in Australia*, The David Elly Press, Sydney, 1980.

——. 'Alexander Charles Kelly (1811–1877)', *Australian Dictionary of Biography*, supplementary volume, Melbourne University Press, Carlton South, 2005.

Hallack, E H. *Our Townships, Farms and Households — Southern Districts of South Australia*, Adelaide, 1892.

Halliday, James. *Wine Atlas of Australia*, Hardie Grant Books, Prahran, 2008.

——. *Varietal Wines*, HarperCollins, Sydney, 2004.

——. *Australia & New Zealand Wine Companion*, 2001 edn, Angus & Robertson, North Ryde, 2001.

——. *Australia & New Zealand Wine Companion*, 1998 edn, Angus & Robertson, North Ryde, 1998.

——. *Classic Wines of Australia*, HarperCollins, Pymble, 1997.

——. *A History of the Australian Wine Industry 1949–1994*, Australian Wine & Brandy Corporation, Adelaide, 1994.

——. *The Australian Wine Compendium*, Angus & Robertson, North Ryde, 1985.

Hardy, Thomas & Sons. *The Hardy Tradition: Tracing the Growth and Development of a Great Wine-making Family through Its First Hundred Years*, Adelaide, 1953.

Haselgrove, H R. *Recollections of a Lifetime in the Australian Wine Industry*, E J Haselgrove, St Georges, 1985.

James, Walter. *A Word-Book of Wine*, Phoenix House, London & Georgian House, Melbourne, 1959.

——. *Barrel and Book: A Winemaker's Diary*, Georgian House, Melbourne, 1949.

Keane, Eve. *The Penfold Story*, W E Smith Limited, Sydney, no date.

Kelly, David. *The Ruling Few, or, The Human Background to Diplomacy*, Hollis & Carter, London, 1952.

Lake, Max. *The Flavour of Wine*, Jacaranda Press, Milton, 1969.

——. *Classic Wines of Australia*, Jacaranda Press, Brisbane, 1966.

Laffer, H E. *The Wine Industry of Australia*, Australian Wine Board, Adelaide, 1949.

Lofts, Graeme. *Heart & Soul: Australia's First Families of Wine*, John Wiley & Sons, Milton, 2010.

Manning, G H. *Hope Farm: Cradle of the McLaren Vale Wine Industry*, Adelaide, 1980.

Mayne, Robert & Gwen. *The Pocket Australian*

Wine Companion, Reed, Chatswood, 1987.

Nesdale, Ira. *The Third Bridge: Tsong Gyiaou McLaren Vale*, Investigator Press, Hawthorndene, 1980.

Norrie, Philip. *Penfold Time Honoured: The History of Dr C R Penfold and Penfolds Wine*, Apollo Books, Mosman, 1994.

O'Neill, Sally. 'Thomas Hardy (1830–1912)', in *Australian Dictionary of Biography*, vol. 4, Melbourne University Press, 1972.

Osborn, R F. *J R Osborn and His Racehorses*, self-published, Canberra, 2001.

Osmond, Robert, & Anderson, Kym. *Trends and Cycles in the Australian Wine Industry 1850 to 2000*, University of Adelaide, 1998.

Pike, A K. 'Young, Adolphus William (1814–1885)', *Australian Dictionary of Biography*, vol. 2, Melbourne University Press, 1967.

Potter, Mike. *Wines and Wineries of South Australia*, Rigby, Adelaide, 1978.

Prest, W, Round, K, & Fort, C. *The Wakefield Companion to South Australian History*, Wakefield Press, Kent Town, 2003.

Pridmore, Adele (ed.). *The Rich Valley: An Account of the Early Life of McLaren Vale*, McLaren Vale Institute Committee, McLaren Vale, 1949.

Roberts, Ivor. *Australian Wine Pilgrimage*, Horwitz Publications Inc., London, 1969.

Santich, Barbara. *McLaren Vale Sea and Vines*, Wakefield Press, Kent Town, 1998.

Simon, André. *The Wines, Vineyards and Vignerons of Australia*, Paul Hamlyn, London, 1968.

Trinity College of Music, London. *Calendar for the Year 1920*, London, 1920.

Warburton, Elizabeth. *The Paddocks Beneath: A History of Burnside from the Beginning*, Corporation of the City of Burnside, South Australia, 1981.

White, Osmar. *A Guide and Directory to Australian Wine*, Lansdowne, Melbourne, 1972.

Zeigler, O L. 'Francis Ernest Osborn, "Bundarra" Vineyards', in *Vines and Orchards of South Australia*, Mail Newspaper Pty Ltd, Adelaide, 1928.

Journal articles

Caillard, Andrew. 'Chester Osborn d'Arenberg', *Gourmet Traveller Magazine*, July 2008.

Dunstan, David. 'With Sam Benwell and the House of Lords journeying to wine in Victoria', *Journal of Australian Studies*, no. 87, 2006.

——. 'A sobering experience: from "Australian Burgundy" to "Kanga Rouge": Australian wine battles on the London market', *Journal of Australian Studies*, vol. 17, no. 2, Winter 2002 (pub. 2004).

——. 'The wine press', in Food and Drink, *Meanjin*, April 2002.

Jefford, Andrew. 'The court of Chester', *Gourmet Traveller Magazine, Waitrose Food Illustrated*, UK, October 2009.

Madigan, Anthony. 'Regional heroes: an hour with the Osborns', *WBM: Australia's Wine Business Magazine*, June 2009.

McIntyre, Julie. 'Camden to London and Paris: the role of the Macarthur family in the early New South Wales wine industry', *History Compass*, vol. 5, no. 2, 2007.

Phillips, Walter. ' "Six o'clock swill": the introduction of early closing of hotel bars in

Australia', *Historical Studies*, vol. 19, no. 75, October 1980.

The Prince Alfred College Chronicle, Prince Alfred College, Adelaide, 1905–10.

The Scotch Collegian, Scotch College, Hawthorn, October 1907.

Wittwer, Glyn, & Anderson, Kym. 'Accounting for growth in the Australian wine industry, 1987 to 2003', *The Australian Economic Review*, vol. 34, no. 22.

Newspapers/trade journals

Adelaide *Advertiser*, 1910–60

Adelaide *Mail*, 1916–1980

Adelaide *Review*, 1970–1990

Adelaide *Chronicle*, 1900–1907

Adelaide *Messenger*

Australian Brewing and Wine Journal, 1923–1960

Australian Wine, Brewing and Spirit Review, 1960–1975

Melbourne *Argus*, 1853–1950s

Bushing Festival Programs 1974–1985

Canberra Times, 1950

English Women's Weekly

Home & Living

Pix, 1958

Southern Cross

Southern Argus

Sydney Morning Herald

Sydney Sunday Telegraph

Southern Times Messenger

The Australian Financial Review

The Bulletin, 1967

The Southern Times

The Wine and Spirit News and Australian Vigneron, 1916–1945

The Australian Magazine

Weekend Australian

Winewise

Winestate

Wine & Spirit Buying Guide, 1980

Research projects and theses

Historical Consultants Pty Ltd. 'The Townships of McLaren Vale and Willunga: An Historic Assessment', Blackwood, 1988.

'Winery Buildings in South Australia 1836 to 1936: The Southern Districts', Architecture Papers, University of Adelaide, n.d., held at Onkaparinga Library.

Woodhouse, Fay. 'A Place Apart: A Study of Student Political Engagement at the University of Melbourne 1930–1939', unpublished PhD thesis, School of Historical Studies, University of Melbourne, 2001.

Interviews with FW

d'Arry Osborn, 29 November 2010 and 1 September 2011.

Chester Osborn, 29 November 2010 and 1 September 2011.

Index

Index